The Bible and Its Message
A Core Course of the School of Leadership

Church of the Nazarene
Mesoamerica Region

Silvia Fernández

The Bible and its message

A book in the "School of Leadership" series.
Core Level Course

Author: Silvia Fernández

Spanish Editor: Dr. Mónica E. Mastronardi de Fernández
Spanish Reviewer: Dr. Rubén Fernández
Translator: Beatriz Alejandra Martinez Riddell
Reviewer: Veora "Cookie" Tressler / Shelley J. Webb

Material produced by EDUCATION AND CLERGY DEVELOPMENT
of the Church of the Nazarene, Mesoamerica Region. www.edunaz.org
Mailing Address: PO Box 3977 - 1000 San José, Costa Rica, Central América.
Phone (506) 2285-0432 / 0423 - Email: EL@mesoamericaregion.org

Publisher and Distributor: Asociación Región Mesoamérica
Av. 12 de Octubre Plaza Victoria Locales 5 y 6
Pueblo Nuevo Hato Pintado, Ciudad de Panamá
Tel. (507) 203-3541
E-mail: literatura@mesoamericaregion.org

Copyright © 2017 - All rights reserved.
Reproduction whole or in part, by any means, without written permission from
Education and Clergy Development of the Church of the Nazarene, Mesoamerica Region is prohibited.
www.mesoamericaregion.org

All Biblical quotations are from the New International Version-2011, unless otherwise noted.

Design: Juan Manuel Fernandez (www.juanfernandez.ga)
Cover image: Yaniv Golan
Cover images and interiors of the covers used with permission under license by Creative Commons.

Digital printing

Table of Contents

Lesson 1	The Biblical Canon	9
Lesson 2	The Pentateuch	19
Lesson 3	Historical and Poetic Books	27
Lesson 4	The Prophets	35
Lesson 5	Introduction to the New Testament	43
Lesson 6	The Gospels and Acts	51
Lesson 7	The Pauline Epistles	59
Lesson 8	The General Epistles and Revelation	67

Introduction

The book series **School of Leadership** is designed with the purpose of providing a tool to the church for formation, education and training of its members to actively integrate into Christian service the gifts and calling (vocation) they have received from the Lord.

Each book provides study materials for one course in the **School of Leadership** program offered by the theological Institutions of the Mesoamerica Region of the Church of the Nazarene. These institutions include: IBN (Coban, Guatemala); STN (Guatemala City); SENAMEX (Mexico City); SENDAS (San Jose, Costa Rica); SND (Santo Domingo, Dominican Republic); and SETENAC (Havana, Cuba). A number of leaders from these schools (presidents, directors, vice presidents and directors of decentralized academic studies) actively participated in the program design.

The **School of Leadership** has five core courses that are common to all ministries, and six specialized courses for each ministry area, at the end of which, the respective theological institution awards the student a certificate (or diploma) in Specialized Ministry.

The overall objective of the **School of Leadership** is "to work with the local church in equipping the saints for the work of the ministry establishing a solid biblical and theological foundation and developing them through the practice of exercising their gifts for service in the local congregation and society as a whole." The specific objectives of this program are threefold:

- Develop the ministerial gifts of the local congregation.
- Multiply service ministries in the church and community.
- Raise awareness of the vocation of professional ministry in its diverse forms.

We thank Dr. Monica Mastronardi de Fernandez for her dedication as General Editor of the project, and the Regional Coordinators of Ministries and the team of writers and designers who collaborated to publish these books. We are equally grateful to the teachers who will share these materials. They will make a difference in the lives of thousands of people in the Mesoamerica Region and beyond.

Finally, we thank Dr. L. Carlos Saenz, Mesoamerica Regional Director, for his continued support in this work, which is the result of his conviction that the church must be holistically equipped.

We pray for God's blessing for all the disciples whose lives and Christian service will be enriched by these books.

Dr. Ruben E. Fernandez
Theological Education Coordinator
Mesoamerica Region

What Is the School of Leadership?

The School of Leadership is an educational program for lay ministry in different specialties to engage in the mission of the local church. This program is administered by the Theological Institutions of the Church of the Nazarene in the Mesoamerica Region and taught both at these institutions and in the local churches enrolled in the program.

Who Can Benefit from the School of Leadership?

It is for all the members of the Church of the Nazarene who have participated in Levels B and C of the discipleship program, and who, with all their heart, wish to discover their gifts and serve God in His work.

The Plan ABCDE

In order to contribute to the formation of the members of their churches, the Church of the Nazarene in the Mesoamerica Region has adopted the plan of discipleship ABCDE, and since 2001 began publishing materials for each of these levels. The School of Leadership is Level D of the ABCDE discipleship plan and is designed for those who have been through previous levels of discipleship.

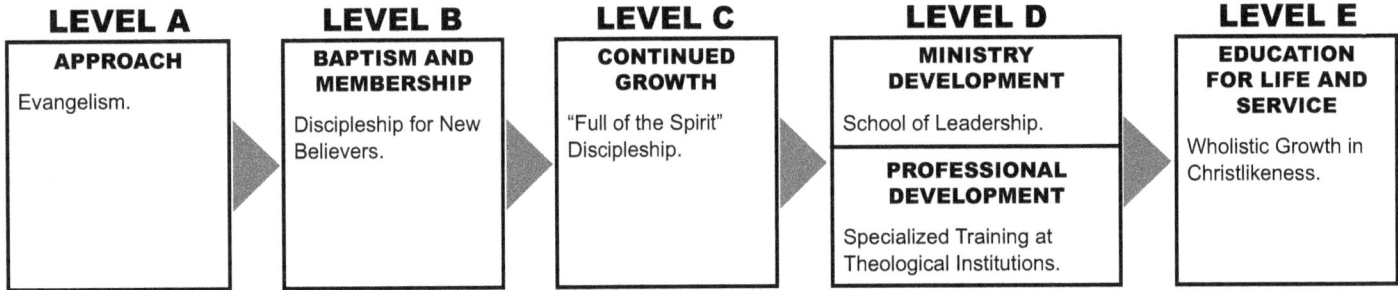

In the Church of the Nazarene, we believe making disciples in the image of Christ in the nations is the foundation of missionary work and the responsibility of leadership (Ephesians 4: 7-16). The work of discipleship is continuous and dynamic; therefore, the disciple never stops growing in the likeness of his Lord. This growth, when healthy, occurs in all dimensions: the individual dimension (spiritual growth), the corporate dimension (joining the congregation), the holiness in life dimension (progressive transformation of our being and doing according to the model of Jesus Christ) and the service dimension (investing our lives in ministry).

Dr. Monica Mastronardi de Fernandez
Managing Editor, The School of Leadership Book Series

How Do I Use This Book?

This book contains eight lessons of the School of Leadership program, along with activities and final evaluation of the course.

How are the contents of this book organized?

Each of the eight lessons of this book contains the following:

> **Objectives:** These are the learning objectives the student is expected to understand at the end of the lesson.

> **Main Ideas:** A summary of the key teachings of the lesson.

> **Development of Lesson:** This is the largest section because it is the development of the contents of the lesson. The lessons have been written so that the book can be the teacher, and for that reason the contents have been written in a dynamic form and in simple language with contemporary ideas.

> **Notes and Comments:** The information in the margins is intended to clarify terms and provide notes that complement or extend the content of the lesson.

> **Questions:** Sometimes questions are included in the margin that the teacher can use to introduce or reinforce a lesson topic.

> **What did we learn?:** The box at the end of the lesson development section provides a brief summary of the lesson.

> **Activities:** This is a page at the end of each lesson that contains learning activities, for individuals or groups, on the subject studied. The estimated time for implementation in class is 20 minutes.

> **Final evaluation of the course:** This is the last page of the book and once completed the student must remove it from the book and hand it in to a course instructor. The final evaluation should take about 15 minutes.

How long is each course?

The courses are designed for 12 hours of class over 8 ninety-minute sessions. Each institution and each church or local theological study center will coordinate days and times of the classes. Within this hour and a half the teacher or the teachers should include time for the activities contained in the book.

What is the role of the student?

The student is responsible for the following:

1. Enroll on time for the course.
2. Buy the book and study each lesson before class time.
3. Arrive for class on time.
4. Participate in class activities.
5. Participate in practical ministry in the local church outside of class.
6. Complete and submit the final evaluation to the teacher.

What is the role of the teacher of the course?

The professors and teachers for the School of Leadership courses are pastors and laity committed to the mission and ministry of the church and preferably have experience in the ministry they teach. The Director and/or the School of Leadership at the local church (or theological institution) invites their participation and their functions are the following:

1. Be well prepared by studying the book's content and scheduling the use of class time. When studying the lesson, you should have on hand the Bible and a dictionary. Although the lessons are written using simple language, it is recommended that you "translate" what you consider difficult in order to help the students understand. In other words, use terms that they can better understand.

2. Ensure that the students are studying the material in the book and achieving the learning objectives.

3. Plan and accompany students in the activities of ministerial practice. The local pastor and the director of the respective ministry must schedule these activities. These activities should not take away from class time.

4. Take daily attendance and grades in the class report form. The final average will be the result demonstrated by the student in the following activities:

   a. Class work
   b. Participation in ministerial practice outside of class
   c. Final evaluation

5. At the end of the course, collect the evaluation sheets and hand them in with the form "Class Report" to the local School of Leadership director. Do this after totaling the averages and verifying that all data is complete on the form.

6. Professors and teachers should not add tasks or reading assignments apart from the contents of the book. They should be creative in the design of the learning activities and in planning ministry activities outside the classroom according to the reality of their local church and its context.

How do I teach a class?

We recommend using a 90-minute class session as follows:

- **5 minutes:** Review the topic of the previous lesson and pray together.

- **30 minutes:** Review and discuss the lesson. We recommend using an outline, chalkboard, cardboard or other available materials, using dynamic learning activities and visual media such as graphics, drawings, objects, pictures, questions, assigning students to submit parts of the lesson, and so on. We do not recommend lecturing or having the teacher reread the lesson content.

- **5 minutes:** Break either in the middle of class or when it is convenient.

- **20 minutes:** Work on activities in the book. This can be done at the beginning, middle or end of the review, or you can complete the activities as you proceed in accordance with the issues as it relates to them.

• **20 minutes:** Discussion about the students' ministry practice that they currently do and that they will do. At the beginning of the course you will need to present the schedule to the students so that they can make arrangements to attend the ministry practice. In the classes when the students discuss their ministry practice, the conversation should be focused on what they learned, including their successes and their errors, as well as the difficulties they encountered.

• **10 minutes:** Prayer for the issues arising from the practice (challenges, people, problems, goals, gratitude for the results, among others).

How do I implement the final course evaluation?

Allocate 15 minutes of time during the last class meeting for the course evaluation. If necessary, students may consult their books and Bibles. Final evaluations are designed to be an activity to reinforce what was learned in class and not a repetition of the contents of the book. The purpose of this assessment is to measure the understanding and evaluation of the student concerning the class topics, their spiritual growth, their progress in the commitment to the mission of the church and their progress in ministerial experience.

Ministerial Practice Activities

The following are suggested activities for ministerial practice outside of class. The list below includes several ideas to help teachers, pastors, directors of local School of Leadership groups and local ministry directors. From the list you can choose the activity best suited to the contextual situation and the local church ministry, or replace these with others according to the needs and possibilities of your context.

We recommend having at least three ministerial activities per course. You can put the whole class to work on a project or assign group tasks according to interests, gifts and abilities. It is advisable to involve students in a variety of new ministry experiences.

Suggested Ministry Activities for "The Bible and Its Message"

1. Have the students form a work group to organize an activity or a special service in celebration of the month of the Bible (September).

2. Have the students teach a class on a topic such as the formation of the Bible or another topic studied in this course. This could be taught to a cell group, a discipleship group, a Sunday School class, a youth group or another group.

3. Organize a Bible distribution day to hand out copies of the entire Bible or the New Testament in schools, hospitals or in another location in the community. Seek out the assistance of other organizations such as the Bible Society or Gideons International.

4. Make models to illustrate the history of the Bible and then hold an event to display the models. The models could illustrate the following: the route that Abraham travelled to Canaan, the route taken by the people of Israel from Egypt to Canaan, the Tabernacle, the Ark, the Temple in Jerusalem, Paul's travels or Jesus' travels, among others.

5. Have the students organize a quizzing competition based on a short book of the Bible or some chapters of a particular book. This event could be for children, teens or young adults.

6. Find or design posters with pictures of Biblical stories to decorate the Sunday School classrooms.

7. Prepare a puppet show to teach Bible stories and present it in Sunday School or in a church service.

8. Have the students organize a contest among children or youth to memorize the names of the 66 books of the Bible in their correct order.

9. Organize a workshop to teach about the Biblical view to a social issue (such as abortion), or hold a seminar about a particular Bible story such as the woman at the well or another story of interest and invite the community to attend. The speaker should be an invited guest such as a Seminary professor or another person who is prepared to speak on the topic. It would be good to begin Bible study groups with those who are interested.

Lesson 1

THE BIBLICAL CANON

Objectives

- To know how the Bible was formed.
- To evaluate the Biblical Canon.
- To understand the meaning of the inspiration of the Scriptures.

Ideas Principales

- The word canon means a measuring rod, rule, standard or measure; it refers to the method used to select the books of the Bible.
- Canon refers to the content of the Scriptures or the books of the Bible.

Canon: A word used since the fourth century "to denote an authoritative list of the books belonging to the OT or NT." The word is from the Greek and means "a rule." (Marshall, New Bible Dictionary, 1996).

The Bible was written over a period of 1,400 years by more than 40 authors from different times and places. Among them are prophets, farmers, fishermen, kings, poets, musicians, doctors, and government ministers, among others.

Introduction

The word canon is derived from the Greek "kanon" and probably the Hebrew "kane" meaning "something used to measure" or "rule, standard or measure." Canon refers to the books that were inspired by the Holy Spirit.

In Biblical language, the canon includes the content of the Scriptures or the collection of books of the Bible that are officially recognized by the Church as books "inspired" by the Holy Spirit.

Formation of the Canon of the Old Testament

The Jews developed the Old Testament collection of books.

Selecting the books that now make up the Old Testament was a long and complex process made by the people of Israel and later by the Christian Church. The sacred text of the Jews is the same as the Old Testament of the Christian Bible, except that some books are combined. That is why the Hebrew Bible has 24 books and the Christian Old Testament has 39.

The books that make up the Old Testament were selected according to the following requirements:

Language: The book must have been written in the Hebrew language.

Age: All books written after 400 B.C. were not accepted because the Jews did not consider anything written after that time to be inspired by Jehovah.

Doctrine: The teachings could not be in contradiction with the books of the Law of Moses (the Pentateuch or first five books of the Bible)

The author had to be known as a spiritual authority to the Jewish people.

The book had to be **widely accepted** by the people of Israel.

There are two dates on the canonization. The first is the year 400. B.C., when it is likely that Ezra and others formed and ordered the writings in a collection of 39 books of the Old Testament. The second was at the Jewish Council of Jamnia, (a town 12 miles south of Judah), between 70 to 90 A.C, where they made official what had long before been accepted.

In both cases, they rejected the books written after 400 B.C. and those in which the author had used a pseudonym or listed the name of another person as the author because the author could not be identified (pseudepigrapha).

The Apocrypha

The word apocrypha means something that is hidden or concealed. A broader definition would be something that is of uncertain value or that has doubtful inspiration. A definition for apocrypha is "writings, statements, etc., of doubtful authorship or authenticity." This term refers to books not considered inspired by the Holy Spirit.

Some of these books have been included in the Bible and accepted by the Roman Catholic Church, but not by the Protestant churches, such as: Tobit, Judith, Baruch, The History of Susanna, The Prayer of Manasseh, and 1 and 2 Maccabees, among others. These books were not accepted because of their teachings in favor of suicide, prayers for the dead, the use of bad means for good ends, superstition and magic.

The Roman Catholic Church accepted another longer canon in the sixteenth century, at the Council of Trent (city in northern Italy) to counteract the movement called the Protestant Reformation.

The Old Testament Manuscripts

The word manuscript comes from the Latin "manus" and "scriptus" and means a handwritten book or paper. The Biblical authors wrote on different materials commonly used in ancient times. Currently there are no original manuscripts from any authors; there are only copies. The manuscripts were classified according to the material on which they were written:

- The Hebrew scroll or parchment scroll: These were used since the days of the patriarchs to the time of Jesus. They were made of goat, sheep or calf hide, sewn and rolled on sticks. It was customary to keep these books rolled. A scroll was a long strip made of papyrus or leather that was reinforced at the ends with two sticks that were used to roll it up.

- The Greek Codex: This was used from the fourth century to the sixteenth century A.D. The codex consisted of bound sheets stitched together to form something like a book. The first one appeared near the second century, but it was not until the fourth century when they were used more frequently. They were written on "papyrus," which was a scroll made from the fibers of an aquatic plant cultivated in ancient Egypt. The rolls or strips of this paper were about 36 cm long and 25 cm wide.

The scribes of the sacred writings were responsible for transcribing the books and did so with great care. They copied the words according to fixed rules and showed great respect for the Word of God. The oldest manuscripts were preserved in the Hebrew language and are called "The Dead Sea Scrolls." In 1947, these were found in the caves of Qumran in the Judean desert. These scrolls contain the book of Isaiah and fragments of other books of the Old Testament.

The Septuagint is a translation of the Hebrew Bible into Greek. This is the version that existed in the time of Jesus, which is quoted in some books of the New Testament.

Johannes Gutenberg was the first to produce the Bible in print in 1455. There were 165 copies in Latin.

Lesson 1 - The Biblical Canon

The Old Testament Versions

The Septuagint is a translation of the Hebrew Bible into the Greek language. According to Jewish tradition, by the order of Ptolemy II Philadelphus (285-256 B.C.), the New Testament was translated by 72 wise men in Alexandria (a city at the delta of the Nile River) for the famous library in the city. This is the version of the story that existed in Jesus' time and that is cited in some of the New Testament books.

The Formation of the Canon of the New Testament

The Canon of the New Testament was completed in the fourth century.

For many years the early Christian Church used the Old Testament as their Bible. While the apostles were living, an official canon was not determined. However, during their lifetimes and under their supervision, collections of writings were put together for church use. These books and letters were placed alongside the Old Testament and were considered the inspired Word of God (2 Peter 1:15; 3:1,2,15,16).

But over time the Church faced certain problems that prompted the formation of the canon of the New Testament:

1. The spread of many apocryphal books, which were rejected by the Church because they contained erroneous doctrines.

2. The heresy of Marcion, who developed his own canon. He rejected the Old and New Testaments, admitting only the Gospel of Luke and ten letters of Paul. His teaching was based primarily on Gnosticism, a mixture of different cultural or religious elements from different regions: Greece, Persia, Egypt, Syria, Asia Minor and others.

3. The heresies of Montanus, which added new books to the canon of the Church and taught new revelations, that according to the followers, were received by the Holy Spirit.

The Books of the Apocrypha

Beginning in the second century, certain books began circulating that did not come from the apostles. These appeared for two reasons. First, they appeared out of a desire of the early Christians to have more information and details about the life and ministry of Jesus and the disciples. Second, they appeared out of a desire to introduce different teachings (heresies) and deceive the people by saying that these writings came from the apostles.

Many of these apocryphal books contain stories of spectacular events, fantasies, and figments of the imagination. For example, some writings explain that Jesus did not have a body of flesh and bone, but that He was

---

Since the apostles were alive during the first century, the words and deeds of Jesus were transmitted orally. The canon became necessary when these witnesses were nearing death.

__Marcion__ (85-160): A Christian from Asia Minor who was influenced by Gnosticism. He taught distorted doctrines, saying that the loving God of the New Testament was different from the cruel and vengeful God revealed in the Old Testament. He rejected that Jesus Christ was the fulfillment of the prophecies of the Old Testament. He taught that matter and body were evil, and he practiced rigorous discipline and deprivation. He denied that Christ had a body of flesh and bone.

an apparition, a spirit, or a ghost. Others gave Mary, the mother of Jesus, a place of greater importance than Jesus Himself, while others taught that one had to stay single, etc.

The following table lists some of the apocryphal books that circulated at the time of the Early Church:

Type	Apocryphal Writings
Gospels	Gospel of the Hebrews, Gospel of Thomas, Testament of the Twelve Patriarchs and Apocrypha of James
Acts	Acts of Paul and Thecla, Acts of Peter, Acts of Thomas and Acts of John.
Apocalypse	Apocalypse of Peter
Epistles	The Epistles of the Laodiceans, etc.
Others	Ascension of Isaiah

Montanism was a movement founded by Montanus between the years of 160 and 170. Montanus called himself a prophet and reformer. He claimed to have direct revelations from the Holy Spirit, received in states of ecstasy. He announced the imminent end of the world and encouraged Christians to gather in a particular place to await the descent of the heavenly Jerusalem. He practiced rigorous disciplines like fasting, deprivation of pleasures, etc.

Factors in the Selection

Between the end of the first century and the end of the second century, gradually the selection and catalog of the books of the New Testament was completed. At the beginning of the second century some Christian leaders came to be known as the "Apostolic Fathers" because they knew the apostles personally. Some of these people were Polycarp, Justin Martyr, Papias and Clement of Rome.

These leaders wrote letters and doctrinal treatises such as The Shepherd of Hermas, The Epistle of Barnabas and the Didache. In these books, they mentioned documents and quoted from documents that the churches had in their possession. These documents had been written by the apostles and so were considered reliable sources, original works of the apostles and inspired by God.

The books that were finally accepted into the Canon of the New Testament had to meet these requirements:

1. Apostolic origin: This means they had to be written by one of the 11 disciples or Paul. The Lord had given these men the responsibility and authority to lead the Church. All the words that came from these men were accepted as if the teaching had come from Christ Himself.

2. Acceptance by the early churches: Paul always wanted his letters to be accepted as genuine; therefore, he signed them with his own hand and sent them with people he trusted and that the church knew (2 Thessalonians 3:17). The Apostolic Fathers emphasized this same thing,

Clement of Rome: The Bishop of Rome during the years 91-100 A.D. He was a companion of Paul, and it is possible that he met John. It is said that he was martyred in the third year of Emperor Trajan in the period between 98-117.

Ignatius of Antioch: One of the Church fathers who lived during the time of the apostles. He was Bishop of the city of Antioch in Syria and was killed in the early second century.

saying that the books must have been received and accepted by the Early Church as coming from a known apostle.

3. Doctrinal uniformity: The books must be in accordance with the teachings of the Old Testament and the apostles.

The Canon of the New Testament was completed in the days of St. Augustine, at the Council of Hippo (393), the Synod of Carthage (397) and the Council of Carthage (419). The Canon, when completed, consisted of 27 books, which were later verified at the Trullan Synod (Constantinople, 692) and the Council of Florence (1441).

The Manuscripts of the New Testament

1. **Codex Vaticanus.** Some scholars argue that this manuscript was one of fifty copies of the Bible commissioned by Emperor Constantine to Egypt and written in Alexandria or Caesarea. It was written in the fourth century and was found in the Vatican Library in 1481, where it remains.

2. **Codex Sinaiticus:** A fourth-century Greek manuscript, which was discovered in 1848 almost casually by a young German named Tischendorf at St. Catherine's Monastery in Sinai. This codex contains the entire New Testament.

3. **Codex Bezae:** Named for its discoverer Theodore Beza. This manuscript was preserved in the convent of St. Irenaeus of Lyon, France for over a thousand years. Beza, a successor of reformer John Calvin, took this important manuscript from the convent and gave it to the University of Cambridge in 1581.

Versions of the New Testament

Having the New Testament when the printing press did not exist was a great blessing, but the problem was that it was completely written in Greek, so that Christians who spoke other languages could not read it. Thus, soon after, translated copies began to surface. Two important translations were these:

1. **The Syriac:** From Syria, the Gospel was brought to Mesopotamia, including locations such as Damascus, Aleppo and Edessa. In the year 150 A.D. the work began to translate the New Testament into the Syriac language, which is very similar to Hebrew and Aramaic.

2. **The Latin Vulgate:** Although the Greek language had prevailed in the Western Church, Latin began to prevail about the year 200 A.D. The areas of North Africa, Italy, southern Gaul and then Spain needed a translation of the New Testament in Latin. Pope Damascus I, the bishop of Rome, commissioned Jerome (between 390-405 A.D.) to translate the Bible into Latin. Eventually the Latin Vulgate was produced. It was accepted at the Council of Trent, which took place between 1545 and 1563.

The Councils had a very important role since they dealt with matters concerning the whole Church. In these gatherings or meetings the bishops discussed and made decisions on matters of doctrine and discipline.

Augustine or St. Augustine (354-430): a theologian and one of the fathers of the Latin Church. He directed several councils between 393 and 419 that were responsible for selecting the books of the New Testament Canon.

Types of Bible Translations:
A Biblical version is a word for word translation of the Bible into another language, although it always requires that the text be meaningful in the reader's language.
A paraphrase is a translation of the Bible that does not attempt to translate word for word, but instead widens the text trying to express what it meant to the original author. It is a more contemporary and conversational style, as if the author were speaking.

How many Bibles are sold annually?
Since its first printing, the Bible has always been the best selling book. In 2008, 578 million Bibles were distributed worldwide.

The English Versions of the Bible

The first English New Testament was published in 1380.

John Wycliffe was born in 1329 in England, where he attended the University, eventually earning his living as an Oxford lecturer and rector (pastor) of two different churches. He was a brilliant man whose lecture halls were always filled with students.

During this time of church history, the corruption in the church was evident and even the king bowed to the bidding of the church leaders. Wycliffe particularly opposed the requirement of having a priest or pope communicate with God for the people, as well as the doctrine of transubstantiation (the concept that the bread and wine actually become the body and blood of Christ). Wycliffe spent time speaking and writing against these issues.

Oxford University finally succumbed to the pressure of the Roman Catholic Church leaders and Wycliffe was fired because of his opposition to these church issues. Then Wycliffe began to feel more strongly that the "people needed the Bible in their own language for a revival to take place" (Wegner, 282).

Although it is likely that Wycliffe had his students help him with the translation work, what is clear is that he oversaw the work of the first translation of the New Testament into English, which was published in 1380. The Roman Catholic Church declared him a heretic for this work.

The Old Testament, translated by at least five persons including Wycliffe's friend, Nicholas of Hereford, was added in 1382. Wycliffe died in 1384. The second version was spearheaded by John Purvey, one of Wycliffe's followers, and was printed in 1388. These two versions were written in Middle English, translated from the Latin Vulgate in a word-for-word translation that made it difficult to understand, although the 1388 version was more readable to the average English layperson.

Translating the Bible into English came at a great price. The Catholic Church did not accept the Wycliffe Bible. "Both Purvey and Hereford were thrown into prison, and some of their friends were burned at the stake with Bibles tied around their necks" (Wegner, 283). Severe penalties were in effect for those who were caught reading this Bible, but this seemed to increase the curiosity of the people. For this reason, "Wycliffe not only gave England the Word of God but also sparked a desire for literacy."

Nearly 200 years later, in 1525, William Tyndale finished the translation of the New Testament into English, although he had been refused when he requested permission from Cuthbert Tunstall, Bishop of London, to do so. He used the original Greek and Hebrew in his translation work, writing in the Modern English period. Since it was not safe to work on the

Preservation and Transmission of the Bible

Up to 2,000 B.C.
• Loose stories transmitted orally from father to son.
• The stories were put into written form.
• Since the time of Abraham (2,000 B.C.), schools already existed to teach reading and writing on clay tablets (Hebrews 9:19).

From 2000 B.C. to 100 A.D.
• More extensive written forms in Hebrew emerged based on oral histories. Later they were made into a book.
• New books were written in Hebrew and Aramaic (the language learned in Babylon and that was spoken in Jesus' time). People began to use papyrus and scrolls.
• In 400 B.C., Ezra and others ordered and formed the collection of the 39 books of the Old Testament.
• The Jewish Council of Jamnia, between the years 70 to 90 A.D., officially accepted the 39 books of the Old Testament Canon.
• They begin to make copies of the books in Hebrew and Greek.

From 150 to 1900 A.D.
• The Canon of the New Testament is completed in 419 A.D. with 27 books.
• The printing press is invented, paper is used, and each copy is identical to the original.
• Translations are written in other languages and copies are made by hand.

From 1900-2010 A.D.
• People try to find and protect the oldest copies of the books of the Bible.
• New translations are available in different languages.

Lesson 1 - The Biblical Canon

translation in England, he moved to Hamburg in 1524 and possibly spent time in Wittenberg, England as he continued the work. When the church authorities heard about the translation, they forbade its printing. In Worms, Germany there was more sympathy for the Reformation, and it was there that Tyndale was able to print the New Testament.

When Tunstall, who had refused to allow the official translation into English, heard of the printing of the Bible in English, he was very upset and bought as many copies as possible to publicly burn. Another leader who was opposed to Tyndale's English Bible was Charles V, the Roman Emperor. He had Tyndale kidnapped and taken from the free city of Antwerp, Belgium so that he could arrested and imprisoned. Apparently the conditions of his prison cell were horrible, since we know he wrote authorities asking for warmer clothing and more importantly to Tyndale, a Hebrew Bible and dictionary. Tyndale was insistent about completing the translation of the Old Testament to English, but in August of 1536 he was found guilty of heresy and condemned to death, and he was put to death in October of the same year. Less than one year later, Henry VIII gave permission for the printing of an English Bible, which was largely Tyndale's translation.

The price paid by Wycliffe, Tyndale and their associates was high. Many gave their lives for the dream of having the Word of God in the English language. We owe a debt of gratitude to these brothers in Christ.

What Did We Learn?

The collection of 66 books that make up our Bible is the result of the hard work and sacrifice of Jews and faithful Christians throughout history, who were guided by the Holy Spirit and who made it possible for us to have the Word of God in our own language.

Activities

Time 20'

INSTRUCTIONS:

1. What is the meaning of the word canon?
   _____
   _____
   _____

2. List the factors taken into consideration in the choosing of the books of the canon of the Old and New Testaments.
   _____
   _____
   _____
   _____
   _____
   _____
   _____

3. In your own words explain what you know about the Apocryphal books.
   _____
   _____
   _____
   _____
   _____
   _____
   _____

4. In groups of two or three, write two reasons why you believe that all that took place to form the canon is an important part of the history of the church.
   _____
   _____
   _____
   _____
   _____
   _____

My Notes

Lesson 2

THE PENTATEUCH

Objectives

- To become familiar with the geography of Palestine.
- To understand the principal message of the books of the Pentateuch.
- To appreciate the history of the formation of the people of Israel.

Ideas Principales

- The Church of Jesus Christ includes all who confess Jesus Christ as Lord and Savior.
- The Church of the Nazarene is part of the universal Christian Church because it confesses and proclaims Jesus Christ.

Introduction

Law of Moses: This refers to the first five books of the Bible, called the Pentateuch or the Torah (Jewish title). These writings relate the beginning of humanity and the people of Israel, as well as the laws and rules given by God to Moses on Mount Sinai.

Pentateuch means a "five-volume book." In the Bible, these are the first five books of the Old Testament. The Jews referred to these books as the Law of Moses. The Pentateuch tells the story of the creation and formation of God's people.

Although the author of the Pentateuch is not mentioned in the books, other books of the Old Testament confirm that the author was Moses (Joshua 1:7-8 and 23:6; Nehemiah 8:1; 2 Kings 14:6). Also, some specific sections, such as Exodus 17:14 and Deuteronomy 31: 24-26 have been attributed to Moses.

The testimony of Jesus in the Gospels also confirms that Moses is the author (John 5:46, Matthew 19:8 and Luke 16:31). Additionally, there are other books of the New Testament that give credit to Moses as the author of the Pentateuch, referring to these books as the law of Moses (Acts 13:39).

Moses had the preparation and knowledge that enabled him to write the Pentateuch. As the adopted son of the Egyptian pharaoh, Moses received the best education of the time, heard the stories of the origins of Israel narrated by the elderly Jews and was an eyewitness to the events of the Exodus and the wanderings in the desert.

To date the historical facts before the birth of Jesus, historians count years in reverse, meaning "Before Christ" and it is written in shorthand as "B.C." The years after Christ's birth are written with the letters "A.C."

The Pentateuch

Genesis	*The beginning*
Exodus	*Deliverance from Egypt*
Leviticus	*Rules for the Levites (priests)*
Numbers	*The census of the people and the period in the desert*
Deuteronomy	*The repetition of the Law*

The Geography of Canaan

Canaan is located in today's Palestine.

The land of Canaan is the place where the story of the people of Israel begins and is known today as Palestine. In the time of the Pentateuch, the territory stretched from the city of Dan in the north to the city of Beersheba in the south (Judges 20:1). It was bordered on the North by Mount Hermon, on the South by the Negev desert, to the west by the Mediterranean Sea and the east by the Jordan River Valley. Based on the characteristics of the Palestinian territory, it was divided from north to south in four regions:

1. The Coastal Plains: A narrow strip that extends from the north to the city of Tyre. It includes the plains of Asher (between Tyre and Mount Carmel), the plains of Sharon (from Mount Carmel to Joppa), and Philistine that goes from the Nile River to the city of Gaza.

2. Western Mountains: These are a series of ranges with a height of 300-600 meters above sea level. This area extends from the mountains of Lebanon in the north to the Negev desert in the south. In the time of Jesus, these mountains were divided into three political regions: Galilee, Samaria and Judah or Judea.

3. The Jordan River Valley: It starts on the western slopes of Mount Hermon. It extends 360 km to the Dead Sea.

4. Eastern Mountains: It extends from the Jordan River to the west desert. In Jesus' time this region was known by the name of Decapolis.

Palestine was the land promised by God to Abraham and his descendants, so it is also referred to as the "promised land" or "land of promise" (Genesis 12:1-5).

When was the creation of the world according to the Jews?
Since ancient days, Jews used a lunar calendar of 12 months that began with the creation of the world on Sunday October 7 of the year 3761 B.C. It is a different calendar than we use today. Today we use the Gregorian calendar that starts from the birth of Christ. To calculate the time of creation according to the Jews, we add the current year plus 3760 years. For example, if we are in 2010 and we add 3760, we would determine that it has been 5770 years since the creation of the world.

History's Origins to the Time of Moses

The book of Genesis tells the story of the first families of Israel.

The narrative of the history of humanity begins in Genesis chapter 1. Although for the Jews the story of human history began 5,770 years ago, Biblical historians have no data that allow them to pinpoint the time of creation. The oldest dates that have been given are approximate and are based on the birth of Abraham in 2165 B.C. (New Bible Dictionary, UNILIT, 1992).

God placed Adam and Eve in the Garden of Eden, a place where they had at their disposal all that was required to meet their needs. God put them in charge of all that He had created. He also warned them not to eat from the tree of the knowledge of good and evil, which they soon disobeyed, making sin a part of the human condition (Genesis 3). With the fall of man, sin quickly spread to future generations and human beings lost the fellowship they had with the Creator. For this reason, God decided to put an end to

Lesson 2 - The Pentateuch

the evil by destroying the people and animals that inhabited the earth by sending a universal flood. Only Noah found grace in the eyes of God, and God commanded him to build an ark to save his family and two of every animal species.

But sin reappears in the hearts of men and women. In the city of Babel, God punished the disobedience of those who organized to build a great tower rather than distribute themselves and populate the earth as God had instructed Noah's descendants (Genesis 10:1-11:9). God "confused their languages" and as a result the people had to divide themselves into villages based on their language and in doing so scattered throughout the earth.

In Genesis 11:27 God sets in motion his plan to rescue mankind from sin and restore fellowship with the Creator. The Lord makes a covenant with Abraham (15:2, 17:2) in which He promises blessing and protection, making Abraham a great nation, and blessing all the families of the earth through his offspring.

Patriarch means "our fathers" and refers to the leaders of the first families of Israel such as Abraham, Isaac and Jacob. The time in which they lived is known as the Patriarchal period.

Isaac and Jacob were the first patriarchal heirs and spiritual leaders of the people of Israel. Joseph was Jacob's favorite son and because of jealousy his older brothers sold him into slavery in Egypt. The brothers lied to their father saying he was dead, but God was with Joseph through many difficult experiences and eventually he became a governor of the Egyptians. Later, through a drought and lack of food, the brothers were reunited with Joseph. Joseph forgave them, and the brothers brought their whole family (70 people) to live in Egypt, in the land of Goshen. There ends the story in the book of Genesis.

Historical Time Period	Event	Books of the Pentateuch
Ancient History: From Creation until the time of Abraham, 2165 B.C.	Historical Beginnings: Creation, the Fall, First Culture, the Flood, Tower of Babel (Adam, Abel, Enoch, Noah).	Genesis 1-11
Patriarchal Period 2165-1804 B.C.	Life of Abraham, Isaac, Jacob, Joseph, Job.	Genesis 12-50, Job
Period of the Exodus 1804-1405 B.C.	Life of Moses, the Exodus, the building of the Tabernacle, the Law, the pilgrimage of Israel in the desert.	Exodus, Leviticus, Numbers, Deuteronomy.

History from the Arrival to Egypt until the Death of Moses

In the days of Jacob, Egypt was the most powerful nation in the world.

Moses was called by God to deliver Israel from bondage.

After 400 years, the descendants of Jacob became a strong and numerous people in Egypt. That is where the book of Exodus begins the story. This population growth caused the Pharaoh to fear a revolt, so he placed them in slavery. In the midst of these hard times, God sent Moses to deliver Israel and bring them to the land of Canaan to establish them as a holy nation and worshipers of the one and only God.

After taking the Israelites out of Egypt through miraculous events, God led the people to Mount Sinai where he gave Moses the Ten Commandments and the instructions to build the first temple (tabernacle). God also gave instructions on how to organize the people's worship and how the service of the priests should be carried out. At Sinai, the Israelites fell into idolatry, building a golden calf. Moses was very angry when he saw what the people had done, and he broke the tablets of the law. Later, the Lord gave the Ten Commandments again and renewed the covenant with Israel.

When they arrived to Kadesh Barnea, God told Moses to send twelve spies into Canaan to survey the land. Upon returning, only two gave a positive report: Joshua and Caleb. Others spoke of how impossible it would be to gain this land because its inhabitants were people of great size and strength. The people believed the ten spies and rebelled against Moses. So God punished the people for their lack of faith, vowing that none of those born in Egypt would enter the Promised Land. Because of this, the people wandered in the desert for 40 years during which time they learned to love and serve the one, true God and live under his laws.

The Pentateuch ends with final speeches, the death of Moses and the appointment of Joshua as Moses' successor (Deuteronomy 27-34).

*The book of **Job** is included in the patriarchal period but it is not part of the Pentateuch because historians located the narrative during the time of Abraham at approximately 2000 B.C.*

Moses: *His name means "saved from the waters." He was a descendant of the tribe of Levi. He was assigned the task of bringing God's people out of Egypt where they were being oppressed.*

God's Covenant with His People

A covenant is an alliance or agreement between two parties.

Throughout history, God has established covenants with His people in which He promises to care for the people of Israel and provide a Savior for all the nations. In the Pentateuch, some of these covenants are listed. Some are conditional and others are unconditional. When a covenant is conditional, God fulfills His part of the agreement provided that Israel fulfills its part. When the covenant is unconditional, God promises to do His part and does not demand anything of Israel.

***Tablets of the law** or **tablets of the covenant:** Stone tiles on which God wrote the Ten Commandments on both sides (Exodus 32:15-16). They were kept in the Ark inside the Tabernacle.*

Covenant With	Biblical Text	Summary
Abraham	Genesis 12:1-7	Promise of blessing to all the families of the earth through Abraham and his descendants.
Israel	Exodus 20-23	Personal blessings promised to Israel with the condition of their obedience.
Israel	Deuteronomy 28-30	The promised land of Palestine promised to Israel forever, but under the condition of obedience.
David	2 Samuel 7:10-16	The throne of Israel forever promised to the descendants of David.
Humanity	Galatians 3:8	Salvation is available to all through Jesus Christ, a descendant of Abraham.

Tabernacle: A large portable tent that people could carry. Artisans developed and stored utensils for worship following the instructions God gave to Moses. It was the sanctuary or holy place for the Lord; the place where God showed himself to the people in the desert. It was also known as the tent of meeting or testimony.

Lesson 2 - The Pentateuch

Literary Aspects of the Pentateuch

Covenant: From the Hebrew "berit" which means accord or agreement among two persons, kings or nations.

Genesis, Exodus, Leviticus, Numbers and Deuteronomy are historical books.

The five books of the Pentateuch belong to the historical literature and law section, since they include legislative writings (laws and ordinances). The following is a brief description of each book:

Genesis means beginning. Its theme is the work of God in creation and salvation. Its purpose is to provide the true story of the beginning of mankind as God's creation, including the fall, the consequences of corruption and judgment, and the introduction to the plan of salvation given by God.

Content of Genesis

Creation (1,2)	Abraham (12-25)
The fall (3)	Isaac (17-35)
The first civilization (4)	Jacob (25-35)
The flood (5-9)	Joseph (36-50)
The dispersion of the nations (10-11)	

Holy: From the Hebrew "qadosh" which means to separate or set apart, meaning that we have been set apart for God.

Exodus means departure. The theme is the redemption and organization of God's chosen people of Israel. The central thought is the rescue and freedom given by the blood. Its purpose is to tell the story of the liberation of Israel from slavery in Egypt and their elevation to a higher position as the chosen people of the Lord.

Content of Exodus

Israel in captivity (1-2)	The Law is given to Israel (19-23)
Israel redeemed (3-15)	Israel worships (24-40)
Israel travels to Sinai (15-19)	

The book of **Leviticus** focuses on the record of laws pertaining to the Levites and their service in the tabernacle. Its theme is the need for cleansing and holiness to approach God. It explains how the redeemed people can come close to God in prayer and how communion with God can be established. Its purpose is to call the people of God to personal holiness. The rituals in the book are used to show the Lord as a holy God and to emphasize that to have communion with Him, you must have the foundation of the atonement for sin and a life of obedience.

Levites: The tribe of Israel who are the descendants of Levi, the son of Jacob. They were assigned the priestly ministry for the people of Israel, possibly because they were the only tribe that did not bow down to the golden calf (Exodus 32:26-29). They did not receive a territory, but they were given 48 cities of Canaan in which to live (Joshua 21:3-42).

Content of Leviticus

Laws related to offerings (1-7)	Laws relating to festivals (23-24)
Laws related to the priesthood (8-10)	Laws relating to the land (25-27)
Laws related to purification (11-22)	

The book of **Numbers** gets its name from the census data that was recorded during this time. Its theme is the organized worship that Israel is to offer to God. Its purpose is to keep a record of God's patience and mercy for His chosen people and that the people would not forget the punishment they received for their sins in wandering 40 years in the wilderness. There are two different generations of Hebrews in the book:

Content of Numbers

In Sinai (1-9)

From Kadesh to Moab (20-36)

From Sinai to Kadesh (10-19)

***Atonement for Sin:** In the Old Testament, the people offered to God sacrificed animals, placing the punishment for personal sin on an innocent victim so that they could be purified. They would pray to God that He would change His anger for a favorable attitude toward the repentant person.*

Deuteronomy means "second law." It contains the final messages of Moses to the new generation, especially focusing on laws they were to obey in their new life in Canaan. The purpose of the book is to keep a record of Moses' words and sermons about the laws that he gave to the people. He emphasized the principles and values that should govern the lives of the sons and daughters of God. These laws should be kept even when living among other inhabitants of the land.

Content of Deuteronomy

History of the People of God (1-4)

Requirements for remaining in Canaan (27-30)

Statement of the foundations of law (5-11)

Final commands (31-34)

The function of the law (12-26)

Generations of the Book of Numbers

<u>The First Generation</u>
• Left Egypt
• Were disobedient and rebellious. As they left Sinai, they complained, lacked gratitude and then rebelled at Kadesh.
• Because of their sins of rebellion and idolatry, they did not enter the Promised Land. Instead, they died in the desert.

<u>The Second Generation:</u>
• Entered into Canaan
• Learned and grew in obedience to God's commandments.
• They entered the Promised Land and God led them to take it as their own land.

What Did We Learn?

The first five books of the Bible tell the story of the creation of the world and humanity at the hand of God. It also explains the origin of the sinfulness of the human heart and God's efforts to form a holy people that serve as a light to the nations that live in sin, in the darkness of idolatry and who are separated from the one true God.

Lesson 2 - The Pentateuch

Activities

Time 20'

INSTRUCTIONS:

1. What does the word Pentateuch mean?
   _____
   _____

2. Write a lesson that comes out of the history of the people of God in the Pentateuch that applies to your life or church.
   _____
   _____
   _____
   _____

3. The theme in the book of Leviticus focuses on the need for cleanliness and holiness to approach God. Does this hold true today? Explain.
   _____
   _____
   _____
   _____

4. In groups of three or four, read the Ten Commandments in Exodus 20:1-17. Then select two or three commandments that represent common sins in children and youth in your context. Choose a familiar melody and then write a song using simple language and with actions included to teach these commandments to children or young people through music. Then each group can share their song with the rest of the class.
   _____
   _____
   _____
   _____
   _____
   _____
   _____
   _____
   _____
   _____

Lesson 3

THE HISTORICAL AND POETICAL BOOKS

Objectives
- To identify the historical and poetical books of the Old Testament.
- To understand the main teachings of each book.
- To learn about the historical development of the people of Israel.

Ideas Principales
- The historical books begin with the conquest of Palestine and continue with the fall to the Babylonian empire and the subsequent restoration of Israel under the Persian Empire.
- The poetic books contain songs of praise and advice for everyday life.

Introduction

The historical books trace the history of Israel from the conquest of Palestine under the leadership of Joshua to the idolatry and rebellion during the period of the kings, which caused the division of the kingdom and the fall of the nation at the hands of the Assyrian and Babylonian armies. These books also tell of the subsequent restoration of the nation under Persian rule. This covers a period of about 1000 years, from the conquest of Canaan in 1400 B.C. to the building of the walls and the temple after the Babylonian captivity, approximately 400 B.C.

The last words of Moses in Deuteronomy chapters 28 to 30 are an excellent introduction to the historical books. In these chapters, God allows His people to see the blessings they will receive if they remain obedient, as well as the curses that come when the covenant is disobeyed.

Mesopotamia: A word from the Greek meaning "between rivers." Located in Asia Minor, it refers to the plains between the Tigris and Euphrates Rivers, where the earliest human civilizations flourished. Now it is the country of Iraq.

Historical Books of the Old Testament	Topic
Joshua	Entrance to the Promised Land
Judges	War with neighboring countries
Ruth	Story of the Moabite woman who became a Hebrew
1 and 2 Samuel	The lives of Samuel, Saul and David
1 and 2 Kings	Solomon and other kings of the captivity
1 and 2 Chronicles	Repetition of the history from Saul to captivity
Ezra	Return of the remnant to Jerusalem
Nehemiah	Return of the remnant
Esther	Hebrew woman who became Queen of Persia during the captivity

The judges were men and women that God called to exercise leadership over the tribes of Israel after the death of Joshua. The title Judge describes two functions: 1) A military leader to guide the people and 2) A civilian leader to resolve disputes and maintain justice.

The Political Climate of Palestine

Idolatry was rampant in Palestine.

Ancient Canaan, today known as Palestine, was strategically located between three continents: Europe, Asia and Africa. This land included the route from Egypt to Mesopotamia, where the great empires of the time were located. Because of its strategic position for military conquests, the kings and rulers wanted to possess Palestine.

Before Israel conquered Palestine, the territory was organized in cities ruled by kings. It was common for these kings to make alliances through the marriage of their children. Although these cities had economic and political independence, sometimes they joined to fight invading armies. Large walls surrounded the cities and outside of the walls there were fertile agricultural fields. The inhabitants were polytheistic, meaning they worshiped many gods. Their main god was Baal, the god associated with rain, war and sun. Their rituals of worship included divination and child sacrifice.

When Israel began its conquest of the two most influential empires in the region, the Egyptians and the Hittites, they found them weakened because of war between the two that had exhausted their resources and manpower. During the conquest, Israel had to fight against those who inhabited the land, who then attacked them stealing everything they had (crops, animals, women, etc.). For this reason Israel had to be constantly on the defensive.

Historical Development

Israel was unfaithful to God and suffered serious consequences.

Jerusalem: An ancient city of the Jebusites and home of the priest, Melchizedek, who was a contemporary of Abraham (Genesis 14:8). Conquered by David around 1000 B.C., it became the nation's capital. It is also known as the City of David.

After the death of Moses, Joshua began the task of recovering the land with the new generation of Hebrews who had grown up in the desert. After crossing the Jordan River, Israel conquered the city of Jericho, and many other cities followed. Finally, the territory was divided among the twelve tribes, who spread out to populate the land. God had given specific instructions that Israel should destroy all the inhabitants of Canaan and not make alliances or marriages with them so they would avoid falling into their sinful ways and idolatry.

But after the death of Joshua, there arose "another generation that knew not the Lord, nor the work which He had done for Israel" (Judges 2:8-10). During this period, the nation was ruled by judges. During the time of Samuel, the last judge, the idea of having a king arose among the people. They wanted the same form of government as the neighboring nations. Thus begins the period of the monarchy. The first three kings of Israel were Saul, David and Solomon.

During the reign of David, Israel entered into a period of progress and expansion geographically, politically, economically and spiritually. The reason for this growth and blessing was David's faithfulness to God. One of the achievements under his reign was to conquer the city of Jerusalem and make it the nation's capital (2 Samuel 5). God promised to establish the kingdom in the family of David through his son Solomon (1 Chronicles 17:11-14).

Lesson 3 - The Historical and Poetical Books

Solomon began his reign well and directed the construction of the first Temple, but he made the mistake of taking many foreign wives (as was the custom of the kings of the time) who brought with them their idolatrous altars and cults. In his old age, influenced by his wives and concubines, Solomon worshiped these gods and the people soon followed him in idolatrous worship. To support all the new construction projects, Solomon charged the people excessive taxes.

Solomon was succeeded by his son named Rehoboam who refused the request of the people to reduce taxes. Rather, he charged the people with more taxes and harder work. In response, the ten northern tribes rebelled and appointed Jeroboam as their king to create an independent nation by the name of Israel with its capital in Samaria (northern kingdom). The two tribes that remained loyal to Rehoboam, the tribes of Judah and Benjamin, formed the kingdom of Judah, with its capital in Jerusalem (southern kingdom).

During the period of the divided kingdom, God sent prophets to the king and the people to bring them to repentance. False prophets also arose and the people often preferred to listen to them instead of God's messengers. For their rebellion and idolatry, both kingdoms were conquered: many were killed and others were deported. In 720 B.C. Assyria conquered the northern kingdom. In 586 B.C. the southern kingdom finally fell under the power of Nebuchadnezzar, the King of Babylon. The city of Jerusalem and the temple were destroyed. This period of history is called the Babylonian Exile.

After these events, the people of the northern kingdom intermarried with the people of the neighboring towns and this mixture of race, culture and religions resulted in the loss of the Hebrew identity (1 Kings 16:4; 2 Kings 17:1-6; 18: 9-11; 1 Samuel 7:8-9). By the time of Jesus, the Jews did not recognize the people of the North (the Samaritans) as Hebrews.

Babylon: founded by Nimrod in 2500 B.C.; the tower of Babel was located here (Genesis 11:1-9).

Babylon was conquered in 536 B.C. by the Persian king named Cyrus. Because of a political change that allowed the Hebrews to return to their former lands, the process of the restoration of Judah began. Many Jews returned to Jerusalem and began to rebuild. The prophet Jeremiah had prophesied that the captivity would last 70 years.

The return of the Jews to their land took place with several groups returning between 536 and 446 B.C. In the year 536 B.C. worship of the Lord began once again with the prophet Zerubbabel. During this time, the Kingdom of Judah took the name of Israel, and rebuilt the city including its walls and the temple. Worship, as well as social and political organization, were reestablished, but under the authority of the Persian Empire. Israel continued to be subject to the empires that controlled the Middle East until the time of Jesus.

Theocracy: a type of government ruled directly by God or by his representatives who guide the people according to God's laws.

After this period of restoration, the next 400 years are known as the "silent period." This theme will be developed in lesson five: *Introduction to the New Testament.*

Literary Aspects

The following is an overview of each of the historical and poetic books.

Joshua means salvation of the Lord. Joshua is the author of the book by his name, although someone else wrote parts of the book. There are several events that happened after Joshua's death: the conquest of Hebron by Caleb (14:6-15), victory of Othniel (15:13-17), and the migration of Dan (19:47). The parallel story is found in Judges 1:10-16 and 18. The theme of this book concerns the conquest and the victory of faith of Israel. Its purpose is to tell the story of the conquest of Canaan and the division of the land among the tribes, and at the same time demonstrate the faithfulness of God who fulfills His promises (1:2-6).

The book of Judges tells of the period of time from Joshua to the first king, Saul. According to tradition, Samuel is the author of Judges. For lack of leadership, the people returned to idolatry and immorality. The tribes suffered at the hands of neighboring villages, although they did have partial military victories under the leadership of the judges. The book's purpose is to tell the sad story of the tribes of Israel during a time when they turned from God's law and to show the need for national unification under the rule of God.

The name Ruth means friendship. Samuel is the author of this book that deals with the topic of love between a foreigner named Ruth and her mother-in-law named Naomi. Ruth's inclusion in the line of David is also a key theme. The purpose of the book is to present the worth of these two women and the virtuous love between them even though they are from two very different countries in an age dominated by violence, war, and idolatry. The book of Ruth traces the genealogy of Ruth and Boaz all the way to King David, from whom Jesus is a descendent (Matthew 1:3-6).

The name Samuel means requested from God. His birth is the result of the fervent prayer of Hannah, his mother. First and Second Samuel were written partly by Samuel, the last judge of Israel. He wrote the first 24 chapters of 1 Samuel. The rest is attributed to the prophets Nathan and Gad. Jeremiah may have compiled the writings of all three authors (Jeremiah 45). The topic of 1 Samuel is the establishment of Israel as God's kingdom. 2 Samuel's theme concerns establishing David as the king chosen by God. The purpose is to present the history of the unification of Israel under a common government, theocracy and rule of God.

The author of 1 and 2 Kings is the prophet Jeremiah, assisted by his secretary, Baruch. The topic of 1 Kings is the glory of the Kingdom of Solomon and the great challenge of idolatry. Second Kings tells of the great judgment of God against Israel and Judah for their acts of idolatry. The book emphasizes the inseparable connection between obedience and blessing, and between disobedience and curse.

Content of Joshua:
1. Conquest of the land (1-12)
2. Settlement of the land (13-22)
3. Joshua's farewell address (23-24)

Date of the Babylonian deportations:
586 B.C. by King Nebuchadnezzar
605 B.C. Group that included 10,000 Jews, among them Daniel
597 B.C. Third deportation

Dates of return to Canaan:
536 B.C. First group under Zerubbabel
458 B.C. Return under Ezra
446 B.C. Return under Nehemiah

Content of Book of Judges:
1. Introduction (1:1 – 3:6)
2. Individual Judges (3:7-16:31)
3. Illustrative Incidents (17:1 – 21:25)

Content of Ruth:
1. Ruth decides to go with Naomi (1)
2. Ruth gleans in Boaz's fields (2)
3. Ruth appeals to Boaz (3:1-18)
4. Ruth marries Boaz (4:1-17)
5. Genealogy from Perez to David (4:18-22)

Content of 1 Samuel:
1. History of Samuel (1-7)
2. History of Saul (8-15)
3. History of David (16-31)

Content of 2 Samuel:
1. The ascension of David (1-10)
2. The fall of David (11-20)
3. The last years of David (21-24)

Lesson 3 - The Historical and Poetical Books

Content of 1 Kings:
1. The establishment of the kingdom of Solomon (1-2)
2. The reign of Solomon (3-11)
2. The breakdown and decay of the kingdom (12-22)

Content of 2 Kings:
1. The end of the ministry of Elijah (1 to 2:13)
2. The ministry of Elisha (2:14 to 13:21)
3. The decline and fall of Israel (13:22 to 17:41)
4. The decline and fall of Judah (12-25)

Content of 1 Chronicles:
1. From Adam to David (1-9)
2. The kingdom of David (10-29)

Content of 2 Chronicles:
1. The reign of Solomon (1-9)
2. The division of the kingdom (10:1 to 11:4)
3. The kings of Judah (11:5 to 36:23)

Content of Ezra:
1. The return under Zerubbabel (1-6)
2. The return under Ezra (7-10)

Content of Nehemiah:
1. The construction of the wall (1-6)
2. The revival of religion and the restoration of worship (7 to 13:3)
3. The correction of abuses (13:4-31)

Content of Esther:
1. The Feast of King Ahasuerus (1-2)
2. The Feast of Esther (3-7)
3. The Feast of Purim (8-10)

According to Jewish tradition, the author of 1 and 2 Chronicles is Ezra, the priest. First Chronicles is about the sovereignty of God in establishing the throne of David. Second Chronicles is about the Lord's reward or punishment upon kings descended from David according to their faithfulness to the law of God or their lack thereof. The purpose of these writings is to emphasize the positive blessings of repentance and sincere worship, and to emphasize the sovereignty of God to restore and keep his promises if His people remain faithful to His covenant. Generally these two books repeat the narration of history found in 2 Samuel and 1 and 2 Kings, although material is added that was omitted in the other writings.

Ezra and Nehemiah wrote the books that bear their names. Ezra recounts the return to Israel of some of the Hebrew people from exile in Babylon. They returned to rebuild the temple and restore worship of Jehovah. This was done at the precise time that God has said it would be done as written in Jeremiah 29:10 (Ezra 1:1). Nehemiah tells of the rebuilding of Jerusalem's wall and the renewal of the covenant between God and his people. The purpose of both books is to narrate the history of Israel after the captivity.

The name Esther means star. The author is unknown but probably is Mordecai (Esther 9:20). Its theme is the continuing care of God for Israel, even in a foreign land. Its purpose is to demonstrate God's sovereignty and loving care for his people. This book also discloses the historical origin of the Feast of Purim.

The Wisdom Books

The poetic books of the Old Testament are these: Job, Psalms, Proverbs, Ecclesiastes and Song of Solomon. These books are classified in different ways: didactic (for their emphasis on teaching), poetry (for their literary style) or wisdom (for their advice giving qualities). Occasionally, all are called wisdom literature because the teachings and instructions that God gives through these books make up what the Old Testament refers to as "wisdom."

Distinctive Types of Hebrew Poetry	
Poetic Drama	It involves a series of scenes, presented mainly in verse as a screenplay (Book of Job).
Lyric poetry	Poems arranged to music to be sung (Psalms).
Didactic poetry	Poems for the purpose of teaching.
Practical teachings	Sayings and philosophical teachings (Proverbs and Ecclesiastes).
Romantic Poetry	Scenes of love in verse (Song of Songs).
Melancholy Poetry	Poems expressing sorrow or lamentation (Lamentations).

The author of the book of Job is not identified. Its theme is the mystery of suffering and its purpose in the lives of God's faithful children. Its purpose is to show how God allows times of adversity to lead his people toward maturity, bringing out hidden sins (as self-justification in the case of Job).

The authors of the Psalms are many: David, Asaph, Moses, the sons of Korah, Etam, Heman, Ezra, Hezekiah, Jeduthun and Solomon. Many of the Psalms are anonymous. The Psalms are poems that served as Israel's hymnal in worship and religious festivals. The book of Psalms has several purposes. The authors express their emotions before God: joy, sadness, disappointment or confidence amid the trials of life. The Psalms also express the hope of Israel in the coming of the Messiah and reveal details of his first and second coming.

The book of Proverbs has several authors: Solomon (1-24), Agur (30) and King Lemuel (31). It is believed that Isaiah and Micah copied other sayings from Solomon for chapters 25-29. The theme is the great benefit of wisdom and seeking God in our lives. The author's purpose is to teach and emphasize the great benefits that result from having a disciplined mind and a lifestyle that pleases God. There are warnings of the great dangers that are a result of being carried away by uncontrolled instincts, passions and desires.

The word Ecclesiastes means preacher or one who talks to a group of people. Its author is Solomon (1:1,16, 12:9). The book addresses the issue of how useless and unproductive is the search for the meaning of life without God. Its purpose is to present a philosophical argument about how inadequate and unsuccessful life is when not living for the Creator. The book seeks to demonstrate the satisfaction and joy of life when one recognizes the sovereignty of God.

The book of Song of Songs derives its name from being the prominent song of all the songs written by Solomon (1 Kings 4:32). Its subject is the delight of love in marriage described in a love story that glorifies pure and natural affection and highlights the purity and sanctity of marriage as a gift from God. Its original purpose was to celebrate the marriage of Solomon with the beautiful Shulamite woman (Song of Songs 6:13).

Content of Job:
1. The attack of Satan against Job (1-2:10)
2. Job and his friends (2:11-31:40)
3. The message of Elihu (32-37)
4. Jehovah's answer to Job (38-42:6)
5. Conclusion (42: 7-17)

Content of Proverbs:
1. True wisdom (1-9)
2. "Proverbs of Solomon" (10:1-22:16)
3. "The words of the wise" (22:17 to 24:34)
4. Other proverbs of Solomon (25-29)
5. Instructions of Agar and his mother to King Lemuel (30-31)

Content of Ecclesiastes:
1. Life without God is meaningless (1 and 2:26)
2. Life without God is unfair (3-5:20)
3. Life without God is unfulfilling (4:1–9:18)
4. Life with God is the only life that makes sense (9:1–12:14)

Content of Song of Songs:
1. The bride in the Gardens of Salomon (1:2 – 2:7)
2. Memories of the bride (2:8-3:5)
3. Weddings (3:8-5:1)
4. In the palace (5:2-8:4)
5. The home of the bride (8:5-14)

The Poetic Books:
- **Job:** Righteous man who suffered and asked the question, "Why?"
- **Psalms:** Hymnbook of Israel
- **Proverbs:** Jewels of Wisdom
- **Ecclesiastes:** Spiritual journey, search for the meaning of life
- **Song of Songs:** Songs of love

What Did We Learn?

The historical books of the Old Testament tell the history of Israel from the conquest of the Promised Land until the exile and return. Although the people of Israel passed through difficult times because of their unfaithfulness, God never abandoned His people and always fulfilled His promises. The poetical books contain hymns, poems and sayings that teach how to worship authentically and live wisely.

Lesson 3 - The Historical and Poetical Books

Activities

Time 20'

INSTRUCTIONS:

1. The Book of Judges describes Israel as a people of God in name, but who practiced the same sins as idolatrous people. Is this a problem in the church of today? Discuss.

___
___
___
___

2. Who were the guilty parties in the division of the United Kingdom into the Northern and the Southern Kingdoms? What lessons can be learned from this history for the church leaders of today?

___
___
___
___

3. What is your favorite Psalm? What emotions are expressed by the author of this Psalm?

___
___
___
___

4. Divide the class into two groups:

Group 1 responds to / or answers the following question: What educational value does the Book of Job have for the Christian life?

Group 2 responds to / or answers the following question: What value or worth does the book Song of Songs have within a context where marriage is going out of style?

___
___
___
___
___

Lesson 4

The Prophets

Objectives

- To define the word prophet and determine the prophet's role.
- To understand the contents of the prophetic message.
- To evaluate the importance of the prophetic message in today's world.

Ideas Principales

- A prophet is someone called by God to convey His Word to the people.
- The prophets served as teachers and preachers.
- There are twelve prophetic books in the Old Testament, and they are classified as major or minor prophets.

Introduction

What is a prophet? Is a prophet someone who predicts the future? Is a prophet a type of psychic? In the Old Testament, a prophet is a person who conveyed a message from God to the people in order to guide them and direct them on the correct path in following God (Genesis 27:27). Some prophets devoted much of their life to this ministry. Others prophesized for a specific time period such as Miriam, the sister of Aaron, (Exodus 15: 20) and Isaac and Jacob, who blessed their sons (Genesis 27:27-29, 39-40, 48:20).

Prophet: A person who speaks to the people on behalf of another. He or she is a messenger of God. (2 Kings 9:7, 17:13; Daniel 9:6)

The prophet Amos said that being a prophet is an assignment from God (Amos 2:11). The book of Jeremiah says that the prophetic mission began with Moses (Jeremiah 7:25). In Deuteronomy 18:9-22, Moses declared that God would raise up a prophetic ministry and that one day the Messiah would be the greatest prophet.

The Function of the Prophets

The prophets were primarily teachers and preachers.

Hebrew Words for Prophet:
Roeh or seer: Describes exceptional spiritual perception that characterized the prophet.
Chozeh: visionary, mystical, contemplative. Describes the life of the prophet, and emphasized how they received messages from God.
Nabhi: Prophet, proclaimer. Stresses the active work of the prophet's message to proclaim God (1 Kings 8:15, Isaiah 1:20, Jeremiah 15:19).

The prophets had the following responsibilities:

• They preached according to the Word of God revealed in the books of Moses and the other existing Old Testament books.

• They predicted future events as God revelated it to them. They warned the people of coming judgment as a consequence of their sin. Likewise, they warned the people of the events related to the coming of the Messiah and His Kingdom.

• The prophets preserved and defended the practice of the Law of Moses. They taught the people and called on Israel to obey.

The prophets are classified as either major or minor depending on the length of their writings. For example, the books of Isaiah, Jeremiah and Ezekiel are much more extensive than the remaining twelve books, which are classified as the Minor Prophets.

The Five Major Prophets	
Isaiah	A call to repentance. Gives promise of the Messiah
Jeremiah	A call to repentance
Lamentations	Mourns the destruction of Jerusalem
Ezekiel	Visions of God's judgment and future restoration
Daniel	The prophet confronts King Nebuchadnezzar. Visions of judgment and the return to the Promised Land
The Twelve Minor Prophets	
Hosea	God's love for His unfaithful people
Joel	The Day of the Lord and devastating judgment
Amos	Denounces Israel for injustice to the poor
Obadiah	Edom will be punished for invading Judah
Jonas	The prophet flees and is swallowed by a fish
Micah	Exploitation of the poor and the perversion of the priesthood
Nahum	The destruction of Nineveh
Habakkuk	The prophet doubts the justice of God
Zephaniah	Judgment on Judah and other nations
Haggai	Encourages the rebuilding of the temple
Zechariah	Visions of restoration and the Messiah
Malachi	Accusations against the priests

Assyria: *An empire that was located in present-day Iraq and Iran. They had a strong army of warriors who dealt cruelly with its enemies. The Northern Kingdom fell in 722 B.C. at the hands of Assyria.*

The Prophets Before the Captivity

The prophetic ministry began in Israel 800 years before Christ.

By the 8th century B.C. both the Northern Kingdom and Southern Kingdom were involved in the idolatry of the surrounding nations, with the approval of the priests and leaders. The books of the prophets of this period are the following:

Jonah (753 B.C.) The name Jonah means "dove." This book has been called the missionary book of the Old Testament, as Jonah is the prophet who preaches to a foreign nation. The central theme is the vastness of God's mercy and the unwillingness of the prophet to preach in an enemy nation. In this book, Jonah declares the universality of judgment and God's grace.

Joel (520 B.C.) Joel means "Jehovah is God." His book is about judgment and salvation in the "Day of the Lord." This is a term used by the prophets to indicate the day or the time when God will intervene in history on behalf of His people. This book has both an historical and a prophetic purpose. The historical purpose includes a call to repentance as the appropriate reaction to the judgments of God in the form of plagues of locusts and droughts. The

Edom: *A mountainous region whose inhabitants were called Edomites. They were descendants of Esau, brother of Jacob. The Edomites blocked Moses and the people on their journey to the Promised Land. (Numbers 20:14-21) The Edomites were always ready to assist anyone attacking Israel.*

Lesson 4 - The Prophets

> **Synagogue:** It means coming together or meeting. Generally refers to a small building used by the Jews to teach the law, worship God and to gather for fellowship.

> *"Remnant" refers to the families of the people of Israel who remained faithful to Jehovah.*

> *Day of the Lord refers to the time when God will powerfully break into history and defeat the enemies of God's people (Isaiah 2:12).*

> **Pagans:** refers to people who practice polytheistic religions, worshiping many gods.

prophetic purpose is to announce the Day of the Lord: a time in which God will submit the idolatrous people to His authority and deliver His people from oppression and dwell in their midst.

Amos (755 B.C.) The name Amos means "burden bearer." Amos prophesized in the time when Uzziah was King of Judah and Jeroboam II was King of Israel. During this time, the two countries enjoyed stability and prosperity. No one suspected that within ten years political chaos and murder would shake Israel and lead to its destruction. The theme of the book is the judgment and condemnation of Israel for their sin, especially their sins of idolatry and social injustice. Amos attempts to warn them of the impending judgment of God upon the nation. He calls them to repent for their socio-economic inequality and their moral and spiritual corruption. The favorite theme of Amos is the righteousness of God.

Hosea (710 B.C.) Hosea means "salvation" or "liberator." Hosea prophesied in the Northern Kingdom for 30 years before he was taken captive during the reign of Jeroboam II (740 B.C.). He was a contemporary to Isaiah who prophesied in Judah. The Israelites had forsaken God and were committing every type of sin and evil. The theme of this book is the inexhaustible love of God for Israel, which produces judgment and eventual restoration. Hosea records the last call of God to the Northern Kingdom before their destruction. He describes the abominable condition of the nation, which is not unlike the prophet's wife who had been sold into prostitution. He also spoke of the infinite love of God who wept over the division of the kingdom and who was ready to receive them again as covenant people, if they would repent.

Isaiah (680 B.C.) Isaiah means "the Lord is salvation." The prophet teaches about national and personal salvation that comes from God. Because of the author's emphasis on the grace of God and the redemptive work of the coming Messiah for all nations, the book has been called "the fifth Gospel." Isaiah warns the nation about the imminent judgment of God due to their own idolatry and alliances with idolatrous nations. He reminds them of the plan of liberation of God for the nation and for each person through the work and ministry of the coming Messiah.

Micah (700 B.C.) The name Micah means "Who is like the Lord?" which relates to the message of the book as it describes the character of the Lord as a righteous judge and loving pastor of Israel. The first chapter emphasizes the power and wrath of God, and the second chapter emphasizes his great forgiveness. Micah describes a people who fulfilled religious rituals but continued in sin and practiced social injustices and violence. The book describes the coming of the Messiah, who from his humble origins, would rule over Israel with truth and justice exactly as God had promised in the covenant with Abraham.

The Prophets Immediately Preceding the Captivity

God warned His people of impending judgment for disobedience.

Nahum (633 B.C.) means "comfort." This book is unique among the books of the prophets because it does not pronounce judgment on Israel. Judgment is directed towards Nineveh, the violent city in the East. Nahum comforts Judah regarding the imminent threat of Assyria and reminds the people of the sovereignty of God over all nations. The prophet predicts the destruction of Assyria as the judgment of God for its violence and cruelty.

The name **Zephaniah** (609 B.C.) means God "hides or protects." Zephaniah prophesied during the reign of Josiah, King of Judah, who undertook a major reform in the temple service. The Kingdom of Judah was coming to its end, and the prophet gives an urgent call to the nation, condemning idolatry and warning about the great day of the wrath of God on the world. He also emphasizes the final results of the judgment of Israel: God would restore them to be a purified and humbled people, and God would once again live in their midst.

Habakkuk (605 B.C.) The name Habakkuk means "to embrace." It is very probable that Habakkuk was a Levite musician in the Temple (3:1,19). He was a contemporary of Zephaniah. The book emphasizes the holiness (righteousness) of God in judging Judah for its sin and using the most feared and powerful nation, Assyria, as an instrument to do so. It also emphasizes that there is hope for the righteous who live by faith.

The name **Jeremiah** (585 B.C.) means "the Lord names or establishes." Jeremiah prophesied during the time when the people of Judah were taken captive and forced to settle in Babylon. His theme is the constant love God has toward his unfaithful people and His sadness for their suffering. Jeremiah demonstrates that the warnings made by previous prophets were to be fulfilled in captivity. Although the sins of Judah had been the cause of the fall, the faithful people of God would be saved and their oppressors would be destroyed. The city of Jerusalem would be rebuilt and the temple would recover its glory.

Content of Isaiah:
1. Conviction for the sins of Israel (1-35)
2. History of the Assyrian invasion, the rescue of Jerusalem and the healing of Hezekiah (36-39)
3. Comfort for Israel and promises of restoration and blessing (40-66)

Content of Micah:
1. The coming judgment upon Israel (1-3)
2. Consolation for Israel (4-7)

Content of Hosea:
1. Separation: Israel, the unfaithful wife (1-3)
2. Condemnation: Israel, the sinful nation (4-13:8)
3. Reconciliation: Israel, the nation restored (13:9-14:9)

Content of Amos:
1. Judgment on the nations (1-2)
2. Judgment on Israel (3-9:6)
3. The restoration of Israel (9:7-15)

Content of Jonah:
1. God's first command to Jonah, his disobedience and the results (1 and 2)
2. God's second command to Jonah, his obedience and the results (3)
3. Jonah's anger and God's answer (4)

Content of Zephaniah:
1. A warning of judgment (1)
2. A call to repentance (2:1-3:7)
3. A promise of restoration (3:8-20)

The Prophets During Captivity

The prophets gave encouragement and hope to the people exiled in Babylon.

Those who were taken captive were given certain freedoms in the Babylonian Empire. However, they had to live under the laws of a foreign nation that served other gods and this brought them difficulties and

Lesson 4 - The Prophets

Content of Jeremiah:
1. The call and commission of Jeremiah (1)
2. General message of rebuke to Judah (2-25)
3. More detailed messages of rebuke, judgment and restoration (26-39)
4. Messages after the captivity (40-45)
5. Prophecies against the nations (46-51)
6. Remembering the captivity of Judah (52)

Content of Habakkuk:
1. The conflict of faith (1,2)
2. The triumph of faith (3)

Content of Ezekiel:
1. The call of the prophet (1-3)
2. The fate of the nation and Jerusalem (4-24)
3. Prophecies against the nations (25-32)
4. The restoration of Israel (33-48)

Content of Daniel:
1. Daniel and his companions (1)
2. God rules over the empires of the world (2-7)
3. Vision of the fate of the people of God (8-12)

Content of Joel:
1. The Day of the Lord, immediate: The invasion of locusts (1)
2. The Day of the Lord, imminent: the Assyrian invasion (2:1-27)
3. The Day of the Lord, future: the final invasion (2:28-3:21)

Content of Zachariah:
1. Visions of Hope (1-6)
2. Exhortations to obedience and to godliness (7-8)
3. Promises of glory through the tribulation (9-14)

persecution. Israel had to adapt to this new situation in order to keep their faith and national identity. The prophets of this period were these:

Daniel (540 B.C.) The name Daniel means, "God is my Judge." At the age of twenty, Daniel was appointed governor of the Province of Babylon. During a period of nearly seventy years, Daniel served six Babylonian kings and two Persian kings. The theme of his book is the sovereignty of God over the kingdoms of this world. Its purpose is to encourage the captive Jewish people and to remind them that God is not finished with the Jewish nation: There is a plan of salvation for the world in which Israel would play an important role. Daniel prophesies that different empires would succeed in the future until the time of the coming of the Messiah.

Obadiah (586 B.C.) The name Obadiah means, "Servant of the Lord." He prophesied in Jerusalem when Edom launched violent attacks against the city. The purpose of the book is to announce God's judgment against Edom and its final destruction because of its retribution and violence against Israel. Likewise, the book proclaims the final triumph of Israel on the Day of the Lord when they would possess the land of Edom.

The name **Ezekiel** (570 B.C.) means "God strengthens." The Jews were practicing idolatry and rebellion. They rejected God and despised the correction of God's prophets. When the King of Babylon captured the most influential people of the Jewish population, Ezekiel was taken into captivity along with King Jehoiachin of Judah (597 A.C.). The house of the prophet became a meeting place where he gave advice to the leaders of his people. The synagogue came about during this time of captivity in Babylon. It was formed by groups of Jews who met to worship and study the Scriptures.

The Prophets After the Captivity

After returning to their homeland, the prophets and the people rebuild Jerusalem and the temple.

The Middle East was dominated by the Babylonian Empire (631-556 B.C.) when King Nebuchadnezzar destroyed Jerusalem in 586 B.C. The Babylonian empire was a result of the union of Assyria and Nineveh, nations conquered by the Medes. In 539 B.C., Cyrus the Persian conquered King Astyages of the Medes, seized Babylon and made it the capital. The Persian Empire remained in power from 556 to 334 B.C. when Alexander the Great conquered it.

The Persians had a different policy regarding conquered people, allowing them to live in their land as long as they paid taxes to the empire. This favored the Jews who, led by God, returned to Jerusalem. The prophets of this period were Haggai, Zechariah and Malachi.

The name **Haggai** (520 B.C.) means "my feast." The book is written when Darius first began his reign and during this time it became possible to complete the construction of the Temple, the work that had been hampered by a decree from Artaxerxes, King of Persia. The work was slowed because of the Samaritans who were feuding with Israel. The theme of the book is the blessing of God in relation to the reconstruction of the Temple and His promise of prosperity and faithfulness. Haggai urges the leaders not to abandon the reconstruction.

Zechariah (500 B.C.) means "the Lord remembers." Zechariah, along with his father and grandfather were in the first group to return to Jerusalem led by Zerubbabel (Nehemiah 12:4,16). He is the only minor prophet who is identified as a priest. This book provides the historical background for Haggai. Both of these prophets encouraged the remnant to be active in the temple reconstruction and emphasized the relationship between being obedient in the reconstruction of the Temple and the blessing of God on their lives (Haggai 1:9, Zechariah 1:16-17). Zechariah encourages the nation to faithfully serve God even in difficult times, placing their hope in the glorious days of the coming Messiah. The prophet wants to prevent them from discouragement since the promises of God have yet to be fulfilled, even though they have returned from captivity. To this end, he assures them that the Kingdom of God will be established and Israel will triumph over all its enemies with the coming of the Messiah.

Malachi (400 B.C.) The name Malachi means "my messenger" and implies "strong authority." The purpose of the book is to awaken the remnant of Israel to recognize their spiritual stagnation. Malachi prophesied to a people who were rebellious and hypocritical. That is to say, they were religious on the outside, but on the inside they were indifferent to the Lord. Worship had become an empty ritual carried out by a corrupt priesthood that was not respected. The promise was that the coming Messiah would judge and purify the nation.

Content of Haggai:
1. Neglect in completing the rebuilding of the Temple (1:1-15)
2. The glory of the second temple (2:1-9)
3. Sacrifice without obedience does not lead to sanctification (2:10-19)
4. The safety and perpetuity of the House of Israel (2:20-23)

Content of Malachi:
1. Admonition and rebuke: messages to the rebels (1 to 3:15)
2. Prediction and promises: message to the faithful (3:16 to 4:6)

What Did We Learn?

The ministry of the prophets was important since God used the prophets to communicate His will to the people in a time when there were no Bibles readily available.

The prophets helped people to acknowledge their sin and repent. They did not allow Israel to forget that God called them to be a holy instrument through which the Messiah would become the Savior of all humanity (Jesus Christ).

Lesson 4 - The Prophets

Activities

Time 20'

INSTRUCTIONS:

1. In your own words, explain what the term "prophet" means in the Biblical sense of the word.
___

2. What are the three main roles of the Biblical prophets?
___

3. What is the similarity between the ministry of the Old Testament prophets and contemporary preachers?
___

4. Malachi, the last book of the Old Testament, ends by presenting the inability of human beings to confront sin when not depending on God's guidance. What has been and is your experience with confronting sin?
___

5. Some students may wish to voluntarily share their response to the previous question with the rest of the class. After sharing, together as a group, develop a list of ten practical ideas or words of advice to help keep our lives free of sin. For example: Be careful what you watch on television.
___

Lesson 5

INTRODUCTION TO THE NEW TESTAMENT

Objectives

- To learn about the history of the 400 years between the ending of the Old Testament and the beginning of the New Testament.
- To understand the context of the New Testament.
- To appreciate the advantages that the Roman Empire contributed to the expansion of Christianity.

Ideas Principales

- The period of 400 years between Malachi and Matthew is called the Intertestamental Period.
- In the first century, the Greco-Roman culture was predominant and Judah was a Roman province divided into different political and religious groups.

Diaspora: *the settling of scattered colonies of Jews outside Palestine after the Babylonian exile*

Introduction

During the time of the Babylonian captivity, the Jews enjoyed a certain degree of freedom. Some served in public office as Daniel did (605 B.C.) while others became skilled merchants. During this time, Esther was chosen as queen and wife of the Medo-Persian King Xerxes (480 B.C.). Some of the exiled Jews managed to overcome their sin of idolatry, which had caused them many problems in the past. This is evident in the experience of Shadrach, Meshach and Abednego, as told in the Book of Daniel.

When the Jews were allowed to return to Jerusalem, some decided to stay and live with their families in Babylon. These Jews continued to practice their religion and meet in synagogues, and they are known as the Jews of the "diaspora." Many years later, these Jewish settlements outside of Palestine were strategic for the expansion of the Christian Church in the first century.

The community of Jews that returned from exile had doubts about re-establishing the descendants of David on the throne of Judah. They held the kings responsible for having brought the country to moral, social and economic ruin as a consequence of the destruction of the temple and the city of Jerusalem (2 Kings 21:10-15, 23:31-25:26). They were also concerned about the need to provide funds to support the temple and its services. Although even Cyrus helped in the provision of the rebuilding of the Temple, (Ezra 1:7-11) the books of Haggai and Malachi indicate that the people were not faithful with their tithes to sustain the ministry of the temple (Haggai 1, Malachi 3).

At the time of the last prophet of the Old Testament, Persia was the dominant empire, but by the beginning of the New Testament, the Roman Empire was the ruling power. To understand how this came about, we will study the history of these two Empires. This will require looking at some of the Apocryphal books of this period such as 1 and 2 Maccabees, which was written between the 3rd and the 1st centuries B.C.

The Intertestamental Period

The history between Malachi and Matthew is very important in understanding the New Testament.

During the 400 years of silence between the Testaments (425 B.C - 4 A.C.), several important events occurred in the world and in the nation of Israel.

Despite the reforms and the religious awakening that occurred in the times of Ezra and Nehemiah, Israel returned to its sinful ways, but this time through religious formalism. They completed the rituals and the sacrifices, but their behavior towards God and other people was incorrect.

Alexander the Great defeated the Persian Empire of Darius III and the Greek-Macedonian Empire took control of Israel (331 B.C). This Empire prevailed until the year 167 B.C. when Alexander the Great died without descendants. The empire was divided among his four generals. Ptolemy inherited Egypt, Lysimachus inherited Trace and Bithynia, Cassander was given Macedonia and Greece, and Seleucus received Babylon and Syria. For a time, Judah was under the rule of Seleucus and later came under the rule of Ptolemy.

Although Alexander had treated the Jews well, the kings of the dynasty of Ptolemy and Seleucus (Seleucid) treated the Jews harshly. In the year 198 B.C., Antiochus the Great of Syria conquered Judah once again. His successor, Anticochus Epiphanes (174 B.C.) did the most damage to the Jews. He banned the worship of Jehovah and killed those who resisted. In 168 B.C. he desecrated the temple by sacrificing a pig (an unclean animal for Israel) on the altar of burnt offerings and dedicated the temple to the honor of the god, Zeus. Antiochus imposed the death penalty on those who practiced circumcision, destroyed all copies of Scripture he could find, and committed many other cruelties and atrocities.

Between 167 and 63 B.C., there was a period of independence due to the revolution of the Maccabees, started by Mattathias, whose family was the most influential during this period in taking back Jerusalem and devoting the temple to the worship of Jehovah (165 A.C.).

Some important changes occurred during the Greek period that facilitated the spread of Christianity throughout the world. It was during this time that a group of 70 Jewish scholars translated the Old Testament into Greek in the city of Alexandria, Egypt (Septuagint Version). The countries around the Mediterranean Sea were united through the Greek language and culture.

In 63 B.C. the Greek Empire was replaced by the Roman Empire, which remained in power until 476 A.C. The Romans, under the command of General Pompey, conquered Judah and named Antipater and his sons as governors of the Jews. They were Edomites, descendants of Esau, the brother of Jacob. Herod the Great, the son of Antipater is the cruel King Herod that is mentioned in the Gospels. He was the governor of Judah when Jesus was born. Herod ruled approximately from 47 B.C. until 4 A.C.

Important People:
- **Cyrus:** (559-529 BC) King of Persia (now Iran), who made an edict permitting the return of the Jews to Jerusalem.
- **Alexander the Great:** Son of Philip II, King of Macedonia and disciple of Aristotle. Because of his military skill, in just a few years he managed to conquer Persia (331 B.C.).
- **John Maccabee:** When his father Mattathias died in the year 166 B.C., he led the Greek Jewish army against Antiochus IV Epiphanes. He conquered the city of Jerusalem and cleansed the temple, consecrating it to the worship of the Lord once again.
- **Pompey:** Roman politician and military leader, who lived from 106 to 48 B.C. He extended the domain of the Roman Empire, and was considered a hero in Rome.
- **Pontius Pilate:** According to tradition, he was convicted in 36 A.D. at Caligula and exiled to Gaul (the land inhabited by Celtic tribes and conquered by Julius Caesar between 58 and 51 B.C.) He later committed suicide.

Zeus: Deity of Greek mythology, the father of the gods who lived on Mount Olympus.

Lesson 5 - Introduction to the New Testament

The World Political Situation in the First Century

Edomites or Idumeans: People descended from Esau, brother of Jacob. They were enemies of Israel until the second century B.C. John Hyrcanus overcame them, forced them to be circumcised and forcibly converted to Judaism. Since then, they have been considered part of the Jewish people.

When Jesus was born, the Roman Empire unified nations from three continents.

In 63 B.C., when Pompey conquered Judea, the world changed for the Israelites. Although Rome respected the beliefs of the conquered people, the desire of the Jews to be free and their assurance of being the only true people of God caused them many problems. The Romans permitted the people under their control to have certain freedoms. In the conquered "provinces" the Romans appointed administrators who were associated through friendships or common interests to the Romans, and this allowed some autonomy for these leaders. This was the situation of Herod and his sons.

The Roman provinces were divided into two categories. The senatorial provinces, which were conquered during the time of the Republic (509 to 27 B.C.), depended on the Senate and a governor named "proconsul." Generally, in these provinces, there was no large military unit of the Roman army because there was peace. In the imperial provinces, there were large military units that reported directly to the emperor. The military were located in remote parts of the empire and were ruled by senators who were appointed and dismissed at the will of the emperor.

The imperial provinces could also govern secondary provincial governments that were ruled by commanders and administrators, but these had limited power. For example a secondary government could not judge Roman citizens such as occurred in the case of Paul (Acts 25). Israel, under the Roman Empire, became the Roman province of Judah and was categorized as a secondary province under a governor, who at the same time was responsible to the governor of Syria.

High Priest: He was the chief priest who ministered in the tabernacle or temple. He was to be a descendent of Aaron in the line of Zadok. He wore special clothing, anointed the rest of the priests and was the only one who could enter the sanctuary on the Day of Atonement once a year. He first offered sacrifice for himself and then for the people.

In the year 6 A.D., Idumea and Samaria came under the direct control of Rome, with a procurator (a civil official of the emperor's administration), dependent on the province of Syria. The Roman administration also extended to include Galilee and Perea. A rich nobleman was named as governor, and he normally would hold this office for a couple of years. This governor had military, judicial and financial power, in limited measure. His residence was in Caesarea, and he had a small military force available to him. One group of soldiers lived in Jerusalem, in the Antonio Fortress, while there were other small battalions occupying various forts throughout the territory. During the feasts or holidays, the governor would go to Jerusalem along with a guard to prevent riots.

In the time of Jesus, Pontius Pilate was the Roman procurator who ordered Jesus crucified. He was not appreciated by the Jews who were angered that upon first entering Jerusalem they had their insignias uncovered and the banner containing the image of the emperor for all to see. On still another occasion he seized the offering of the Temple with which he ordered the building of an aqueduct.

The Law of Moses was recognized as state law for all Jews, including those residing in Palestine and those spread throughout the Roman Empire. The Sanhedrin was the institution that served as a court of justice, but only the Roman governor could pass the death sentence. The Sanhedrin was composed of 71 members chosen from among the elders, priests and Pharisees.

In today's world, we too have different religious groups. Which religious groups are most common in the town or city where you live?

All Jews were required to pay taxes and fees to the imperial treasury. These were collected by the "publicans," who were Jews employed by Rome, for which they were considered traitors. However, the Jews were not required to participate in the worship of the gods of the Empire, including worship of the Emperor, out of respect of their religion. The Jewish priests, who offered sacrifices in the morning and the evening, conducted the temple worship. The only thing the Romans did that showed their disrespect regarding Jewish worship was that the governor named and appointed the High Priest.

The worship of the emperor *required the worship of the living emperor and also the Roman emperors who had died. They were considered gods.*

In the time of Jesus, Judah was bordered to the North by the province of Samaria. The Samaritans were Jews who intermarried with idolatrous people during the exile of Israel. Because of their racial and religious mix, the Jews in the time of Nehemiah did not permit the Samaritans to participate in the reconstruction of the Temple. This was the reason the Samaritans constructed their own temple on the Mount of Gerizim, which caused more tension between the Jews and Samaritans.

Why is it important to understand the world in which the New Testament was written?

Herod the Great, King of the Jews

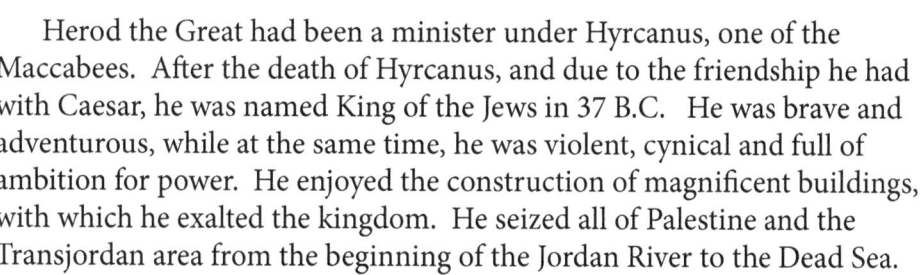

In the time of Jesus' birth, the Jews were ruled by an idolatrous, foreign king.

Herod the Great had been a minister under Hyrcanus, one of the Maccabees. After the death of Hyrcanus, and due to the friendship he had with Caesar, he was named King of the Jews in 37 B.C. He was brave and adventurous, while at the same time, he was violent, cynical and full of ambition for power. He enjoyed the construction of magnificent buildings, with which he exalted the kingdom. He seized all of Palestine and the Transjordan area from the beginning of the Jordan River to the Dead Sea. He founded the port of Caesarea on the Mediterranean and established businesses along the Red Sea.

Besides Caesarea, Herod rebuilt Samaria and restored Jerusalem, building an aqueduct, the new temple and restoring the tombs of the patriarchs. Other constructions for which he was responsible were these: the Tower of Antonia, the Fortresses of Masada, Herodion and Machaerus. He also built a new royal palace that was fortified with three towers.

Roman Legion: a military term used in the Roman army that refers to an elite group of up to 6,000 Roman soldiers.

Despite all the good things he did, the Jews hated him for various reasons:

- He was not Jewish, but Edomite. The Edomites had always been enemies of Israel.

Galilee: The region to the north of Israel that had a mixed population. Almost all the disciples, like Jesus, came from this region.

- He had good relations with Rome.

- He established places of worship to the emperor in various Jewish cities.

- He did not respect the authority of the Sanhedrin, the religious leaders of Israel or the law of Moses.

- He killed his own sons, Alexander and Aristobulus, his wife Mariamne, and even left orders to execute many nobles at his death so there would be many people crying and mourning at his funeral.

- He commanded the killing of the male children in Bethlehem in an attempt to destroy the Messiah.

Caesarea: A city built by Herod in honor of Caesar Augustus on the coast of Judea (104 km northwest of Jerusalem).

The Political / Religious Groups in Palestine

Religious diversity in the 1st century was similar to our postmodern world.

In the first century in Palestine, religion occupied a very important place and was closely related to social and political issues. The same people exercised both political and religious authority. There were a variety of religious groups with which Jesus interacted. He conversed with them and chastised them publically for abusing their power and authority.

The **Pharisees,** whose name means "separated," were priests who lived according to the traditions and laws of Moses. They were strict especially regarding the ceremonial laws of purification as described in Leviticus, chapters 11 to 16. The Pharisees were important to Israel because they were the defenders of Jewish tradition, and they opposed any new ideas or teachings that attempted to follow Greek culture.

Circumcision: From the time of Abraham (Genesis 17:24), the men of Israel cut the skin covering of the penis, called the foreskin. This ritual was adopted as an outward sign of the covenant.

In the 2nd century B.C., a division emerged among the Pharisees and the **Sadducees,** consisting of priests and elders who opposed the Pharisees. The Sadducees were very strict in their doctrinal beliefs and had their own criminal code. They were very influential due to their economical power.

During the same time period that the Sadducees began, the **scribes** became yet another sect or group. The scribes were priests who were specialists in the interpretation of the Law. They were part of a lower class than the Pharisees and the Sadducees. The power of the scribes was in their knowledge, which they acquired through many years of study. They were called, Rabbi, which means, teacher. They were the only priests authorized as instructors of doctrine. Their education allowed them to work as teachers, administrators and lawyers. All members of the Sanhedrin that were scribes, were at the same time, Pharisees.

The word "Sanhedrin" means "sit together." This group was formed by 71 of the leading men of Israel: priests, nobles and scribes. The High Priest presided over the Sanhedrin. The group administered justice in civil and religious affairs.

The **Zealots** formed a group of political resistance against the Roman Empire. They were primarily responsible for the rebellion that would lead to the destruction of Jerusalem in 70 A.D. It is likely that one of the disciples of Jesus was a Zealot (Luke 6:15). The **Herodians** were a political group that favored King Herod. The alliance of this group and the Pharisees to destroy Jesus can be seen in the history narrated in the Gospels.

The Essenes formed their own spiritual community, which was very strict in its rules and regulations. They practiced voluntary denial of pleasures such as eating, rest, comfort, sex, among others. They were very severe in their conduct and did not give rise to anger, kept the Sabbath with great rigidity and were very careful in their personal hygiene. They resembled the Pharisees in their strict adherence to the law.

The Greco-Roman World and the Spread of Christianity

The first century world stage was key to the spread of the gospel.

The first century civilization is called Greco-Roman because it was influenced mainly by the Greek and Roman cultures. The ideas and customs of the conquered peoples were slowly disappearing, and they were adopting the customs of the Greeks and Romans. Even the Jews of Palestine, despite their great zeal for the teachings of their parents, had adopted Greek philosophical thought and new ways of living.

Although the Romans established political and administrative principles of the empire, it was Greek philosophy and thought that molded the intellectual life. Greek culture dominated the civilized world. In other words, the world belonged to the Romans, politically speaking, but Greek culture dominated. The religion was polytheistic and the people could choose from a variety of Greek gods, emperor worship and religions of the East.

The Roman Empire and its Advantages to the Spread of Christianity
• Speed of communication: the news spread rapidly throughout the empire.
• Roman roads and trade routes were constructed throughout the entire empire, making travel easier and safer to various regions.
• Large cities existed that Paul strategically chose as locations to begin new churches, and from there the word was spread to the smaller towns.
• Commerce flourished and was enjoyed by all. There was a certain level of economic prosperity that allowed people the time to consider spiritual topics.
• Rome adopted the culture and philosophy of Greece. The Greek culture and its focus on intellect had a great influence in world history. The Greek language was established as the universal language and allowed greater diffusion of the teachings of Jesus.
• Polytheism could not meet the spiritual needs of the people. The influence of Eastern religions gave a spiritual hunger to the people to know the one true God. Christianity took advantage of this opportunity to spread the news of the one true God.

What Did We Learn?

God sent his Son at the perfect moment in history, so that he would give testimony to Israel before its destruction in the year 70 A.D. and in order to establish the Christian Church. In the first century, the Roman Empire provided the opportunity for the spreading of the message of salvation throughout the entire Roman Empire.

Activities

Time 20'

INSTRUCTIONS:

1. What was the positive result of the Babylonian captivity for the people of Israel?
_____
_____
_____

2. What was the spiritual condition of the Jewish people at the time of Jesus' birth?
_____
_____
_____

3. In your opinion, how were the religious leaders of Israel carrying out their roles?
_____
_____
_____

4. Work in groups of three or four to identify the aspects of the Roman Empire that favored the spread of Christianity, and identify any similarities with our present world and its globalization.

The Roman Empire of the First Century	Twenty First Century World

5. Working in the same groups, answer the following questions:
a) Is this an opportune time for the spreading of the gospel?
b) What opportunities should the Church of the twenty-first century take advantage of?
_____
_____
_____
_____
_____

Lesson 6

THE GOSPELS AND ACTS

Objectives

- To understand the general characteristics of the Gospels and Acts.
- To identify the principle purpose of each book.
- To appreciate the message of these books for today.

Ideas Principales

- The four Gospels tell the story of the life and teaching of Jesus.
- The book of Acts gives us the history of the first Christians.
- Matthew, Mark and Luke are called "Synoptic Gospels" because they are similar in order and content.

Introduction

The first three Gospels are called synoptic because they all provide a synopsis (or summary). They basically follow the same pattern as they narrate the events surrounding the life of Jesus. Some argue that the similarities exist because Luke and Matthew used the Gospel of Mark as their source, which was the first Gospel to be written. The format of the Gospel of John is different from that of the Synoptic Gospels.

The first three Gospels are referred to as the "Synoptic" Gospels.

What are the differences between the Synoptics and the Gospel of John?

- The Synoptic Gospels tell the story of Jesus to non-Christians for evangelistic purposes. John, however, wrote to edify Christians and the Church.

- In the Synoptics, more detail is given to the ministry of Jesus in Galilee, while John focuses more on his ministry in Judea.

- In the first three gospels, more is said about the public life of Jesus, whereas John writes more about his private life.

- The Synoptic Gospels emphasize the authentic and perfect humanity of Christ. The fourth gospel reveals the great and genuine divinity of Christ.

Why Are There Four Gospels?

The possible reasons for having four gospel accounts.

Several reasons can be mentioned as to why there are four gospels:

First, each of the evangelists wrote to different groups of people. Matthew wrote to the Jews; therefore, in his gospel, he presents Jesus as the Messiah. Mark wrote to the Romans, a people whose ideal was power and service to the Empire; consequently, he presents Christ as a powerful conqueror. Luke wrote to the Greeks who idealized the perfect man and for that reason he presents Christ as the expression of this ideal. John has in mind the needs of Christians of all nations, and he writes to the Church presenting the most profound truths of the gospel.

Second, a single gospel was not enough to present the many aspects of the person of Christ. Third, the evangelists wrote their narratives from different points of view. That explains the differences between their accounts: omissions, additional details that each of them provides, and apparent occasional "contradictions" and differences in the chronological order of events.

Finally, these writers were not attempting to write a complete biography of the life of Christ; rather, their motivation was to satisfy the needs of the people to whom they wrote. For this reason, they chose the incidents and teachings that would emphasize what they were seeking to portray regarding Jesus' life. For example, Matthew, writing to Jews, selected the events that gave emphasis to the messianic mission of Jesus.

Literary Aspects of the Gospels

Now we will learn about the authorship, date, setting, etc. of the Gospels.

Understanding the literary aspects of each Gospel helps us to distinguish them.

When we speak of literary aspects of the different books of the Bible, we refer to matters that have to do with authorship, date, setting, recipients, and author's purpose, among others. Knowing this information contributes to a better understanding of each book.

Matthew is the gospel that presents Jesus as the Messiah King. Its author, Matthew, was a tax collector under Roman rule. Tradition says that Matthew preached in Palestine a few years and then visited other countries. The book is dated between 60 and 70 A.D.

The recipients of this book are Jews. Matthew, knowing their great expectations, depicts Jesus as the Messiah, whose coming had been anticipated by the prophets of Israel. The prophecy of the Old Testament ends with the promise of a king who was to come to Israel. The purpose of this gospel is to prove that Jesus was the King. But the Jews who rejected him would also be rejected of any divine favor. Matthew used about sixty references from the Old Testament as proof for his writing.

Mark presents Jesus in his Gospel as the mighty conqueror. Mark was the son of Mary, a woman of Jerusalem, whose home was open to Christians (Acts 12:12). He accompanied Paul and Barnabas on their first missionary journey, but later he returned to Jerusalem. This did not please Paul, who later refused to take Mark with him. This caused Barnabas to separate from Paul and take Mark with him to Cyprus (Acts 15:36-41). Mark was successful in his ministry, being mentioned in 1 Peter 5:13. Paul later changed his opinion regarding Mark (2 Timothy 4:11). The testimony of the church fathers indicates that Mark accompanied Peter to Rome as his interpreter, and Mark compiled his gospel from Peter's preachings.

Content of Matthew
1. The arrival of the Messiah (1:1 to 4:11)
2. The ministry of the Messiah (4:12 to 16:12)
3. The claim of the Messiah (16:13 to 23:39)
4. The sacrifice of the Messiah (24-27)
5. The triumph of the Messiah (28)

Content of Mark
1. The coming of the great conqueror (1-2:12)
2. The conflict of the powerful King (2:13 to 8:21)
3. His right to the realm of power (8:31 to 13:37)
4. Preparation for the establishment of the Kingdom (14 to 15:47)
5. Jesus and His spiritual kingdom (16)

Content of Luke
1. Introduction (1:1-4)
2. Arrival of the divine man (1:5 to 4:13)
3. Ministry in Galilee (4:14 to 9:50)
4. Ministry in Perea (9:51 to 19:28)
5. Crucifixion and resurrection (19:29 to 24:53)

Content of John
1. Preface (1:1-18)
2. The revelation of Christ to the world (1:19 to 6:71)
3. The rejection of Christ (7:1 to 12:50)
4. The manifestation of Christ to his disciples (13 to 17)
5. The humiliation and glorification of Christ (18 to 21)

The Temple Moneychangers:
In Jesus' time people needed to exchange money because in the temple it was not acceptable to give an offering or to buy animals for sacrifice using foreign money. The moneychangers cheated people who came to worship by giving them an exorbitant exchange rate for their money. Jesus renounced these Jewish merchants who were in conspiracy with the priesthood of the time and who became rich by taking advantage of the people.

The Gospel of Mark was written between 60 and 70 A.D. for the Romans, a proud people, who glorified in the supremacy of their armies. Mark gives special prominence to the miracles of Jesus as a manifestation of His superhuman power. He presents the works of Christ as the Redeemer of mankind sent by the Father, so that humanity would believe in the one and only true God. In his gospel he demonstrates that Jesus did not come just for the Jews but for the people of all nations.

In his gospel account, **Luke** presents Jesus as the perfect human who is also divine. Luke was a Greek physician and companion of Paul. Christian writers of the first centuries indicate that the Gospel of Luke was essentially what Paul and Luke preached among the Greeks and that was distributed among the Greeks in 63 A.D. The Greeks were obsessed with the perfection of the human being in the moral, intellectual and physical aspects. Luke presents Jesus as the ideal man, perfect and complete. In his gospel, Luke demonstrates that Jesus came to save all men through His death.

The Gospel of **John** presents Jesus as the Son of God. The book was written in the year 90 A.D. In his gospel, John exposes the profound truths he learned as the disciple closest to Jesus. He writes for Christians throughout the entire Roman Empire who longed to know the most profound truths of the gospel. John presents Christ as the Word made flesh, the Son of God (John 20:31). Unlike the Synoptics that tell the story of Jesus using facts, John provides a spiritual interpretation.

Evans (1990, p. 97) provides a comparative summary of the focus of each of the four Gospels:

Gospel	Directed to	Main Point	Writing Focus	Central Thought	Prominent Word
Matthew-King	Jews	Jesus the Messiah King	Speeches	Kingship	Fulfilled
Mark-Servant	Romans	Jesus, Servant of God	Miracles	Service	Immediately
Lucas-Man	Greeks	Jesus the perfect Son of Man	Parables	Humanity	Compassion
John-Godhead	Christians	Jesus, Divine Son of God	Speeches	Divinity	Believe

The Life of Jesus

Jesus came to fulfill the mission entrusted to Him by His Father.

Jesus was born before the death of Herod, which occurred in 4 B.C. and near the time of the census ordered by Caesar Augustus, between 7 to 4 B.C. Therefore, Jesus was born between 4 and 5 B.C. and not in the 1

A.D. of our era. It was not until 600 years after the birth of Jesus that his birth was recognized as an event. Dionysius Exigus, using information he had at the time, counted the years back and established what he believed to have been the exact date of Jesus' birth. Based on his calculations, the Christian calendar was established that is still in use today. It was not until centuries later, after a recalculation, that the error was discovered, but it was impossible then to change the calendar.

In the early childhood of Jesus, his parents Joseph and Mary had to flee to Egypt to save his life. When the danger passed, they returned and settled in Nazareth. From that time on, there are no other records of the childhood years of Jesus, except the incident in the temple as recorded in Luke 2:41-52. Luke 2:52 says: "And Jesus grew in wisdom and stature, and in favor with God and man."

The ministry of Jesus begins when he presented himself to John the Baptist at the Jordan River to be baptized. Later, he was taken to the desert by the Holy Spirit. Matthew (4:1-11), Mark (1:12-13), and Luke (4:1-13) present a dramatic dialog between Jesus and Satan in the wilderness where Jesus decisively rejects the three proposals put to him by the devil by quoting Deuteronomy 6:13, 16, and 8:3. After returning from the desert, Jesus calls his first disciples (John 1:35-51), performs several miracles in Galilee and Jerusalem (John 2 and 3) and then travels to Samaria (John 4:1-42).

When John the Baptist was in prison, Jesus began an extensive ministry of teaching and healing in Galilee, and consequently He became popular. His message was to announce that the Kingdom of God had arrived and was for all people (Mark 1:14). To be a part of the Kingdom, one had to repent of sin, and this news was not gladly accepted by all. For example, in the synagogue of Nazareth the people threw him out of the city (Luke 4:16-30) and forced him to move his ministry base to Capernaum. From there Jesus took his ministry to all parts of Galilee for more than a year, (Mark 1:14 – 6:34, John 4:46-54) demonstrating his power over nature, (Mark 4:35-41, 6:34-51) demons, (Luke 8:26-39, 9:37-45) diseases (Matthew 8:1-17, 9:1-8) and even over death (Matthew 9:18-26, Luke 7:11-17).

The Passover Meal: *This refers to the food that was prepared during the week of Passover in preparation for the meal, which consisted of roast lamb, bitter herbs, unleavened bread and grape juice in commemoration of the deliverance of Israel from Egypt. This was the last meal Jesus ate with his disciples, and it became the establishment of the Sacrament of the Lord's Supper.*

The Sermon on the Mount (Matthew 5-7) is a good compilation of the doctrine that Jesus taught. In this sermon, Jesus claimed to have full authority in the interpretation of the Old Testament. He also revealed his love and compassion for the distressed and oppressed (Matthew 9:1-8, 18-22, Luke 8:43-48). On many occasions Jesus stated that he had come to seek and save the lost, and he exercised his divine authority to forgive sins (Luke 5:20-26).

Regarding the preparation of the disciples, Jesus chose twelve men (Matthew 10:1-4) and spent time preparing them to be his apostles. He used a variety of techniques in his teaching including parables, discussion, direct teaching and his constant personal example.

Feast of Pentecost: The celebration that took place for the fifty days after the resurrection and ended with the day of Pentecost. This commemorated the date when Israel received the Law of Moses in the desert, fifty days after leaving Egypt.

Jesus had to face enemies throughout his ministry. The opposition of the political rulers and the religious teachers of the Jews grew rapidly (Luke 14:1). It was their desire to find fault with Jesus in order to accuse him, damage his reputation with the multitudes that followed him, and eventually have him put to death by the Roman authorities (Matthew 19).

In the last week before his crucifixion, Jesus entered Jerusalem as the long awaited Messiah, cheered on by the crowds (Mark 11:1-10). Under his authority as the Messiah, He went to the temple and drove out the moneychangers who sold animals for sacrifice. In the days following, He dedicated himself to teaching in the temple and preparing his disciples for his death and resurrection. He also prophesized the sad end that awaited the city of Jerusalem and its inhabitants, and He spoke about the signs of his second coming as the King of Kings and Lord of Lords (Matthew 24 and 25).

The prophecy of Jesus concerning the destruction of Jerusalem, found in Matthew 24 and 25, was fulfilled in 70 A.D. when the Roman General Titus destroyed the city.

Before he was arrested, Jesus washed the disciples' feet (John 13:1-17) and announced that Judas would betray Him (Mark 14:18-21). That night he instituted the Lord's Supper (Mark 14:22-25) and taught his disciples many lessons (John 13-17). After they had eaten, they went to the Garden of Gethsemane, where Jesus agonized and struggled in prayer and gave himself unreservedly to the will of the Father. He allowed himself to be arrested, abused and wrongfully convicted before the Sanhedrin and finally crucified. His torture culminated on the cross after several hours of agony (Mark 15:34).

This was the mission for which he had come, "to give his life a ransom for many" (Mark 10:45) delivering himself into the hands of God, knowing that the work entrusted to him by the Father had been fulfilled (Luke 23:46, John 19:30). Friends took his body from the cross and buried him. On the third day, early on Sunday morning, the women who went to the tomb found it empty (Mark 16).

That same day Jesus appeared alive to many of his followers, giving evidence of His resurrection (Matthew 29:9-10, Luke 24:13-31, John 20:11-21.22). In the following forty days, Jesus appeared various times, especially to his disciples to give them new teachings about correctly interpreting the Old Testament, the coming of the Holy Spirit, the mission to the world and being prepared to serve as spiritual leaders in the new church (Luke 24:51, Acts 1: 9-11). Days after the ascension of Jesus, the Holy Spirit filled the hearts of the 120 disciples gathered on the day of the feast of Pentecost, which was the beginning of the ministry of the Christian Church.

The Acts of the Apostles

Early Christian history gives us a worthy model to follow.

This book tells about the expansion of the Church from Jerusalem to Rome, the capital of the empire. A portion of the book is dedicated to the ministry of Peter. However, the majority of the book relates the ministry of Paul as he travels and establishes churches throughout many of the provinces in the area of the Mediterranean Sea.

Luke is the author, and he likely wrote the account in the year 63 A.D., two years after Paul's imprisonment in Rome. He writes about the establishment and growth of the Christian Church and the proclamation of the good news of the gospel to the known world at that time. The purpose of the book is to demonstrate how the Church, founded by Christ, developed in its early stages as guided by the Holy Spirit. The book of Acts, which exhibits the character, principles and purposes of the Church, was written particularly to Theophilus, but overall to the entire Church.

Content of Acts
1. The Church in Jerusalem (1 to 8:4)
2. The Church in Palestine and Syria (8:5 to 12:23)
3. The Church of the Gentiles (12:24 to 21:17)
4. The final scenes in the life of Paul (21:18-28:31)

The Events of the Life of Jesus Christ in the Four Gospels

Gospels	Matthew	Mark	Luke	John
The Pre-Incarnate Christ				1:1-3
His birth and childhood	1,2		1,2	
John the Baptist	3:1 - 12	1:1 - 8	3:1 - 20	1:6 - 42
Baptism of Jesus	3:13 - 17	1:9 - 11	3:21 - 22	
The Temptation	4:1 - 11	1:12 - 13	4:1- 13	
The first miracle				2:1 - 11
Beginning of ministry in Judea (about 8 months)				2:13 to 4:3
Visit to Samaria				4:4 - 42
Ministry in Galilee (about 2 years)	4:12 to 19:1	1:14 to 10:1	4:14 to 9:51	4:43 -54 and 6:1 - 7:1
Ministry in Perea and Judea (about 4 months)	19 and 20		9:51 to 19:28	7:2 to 11:57
The Passion Week	21 - 27	11 - 15	19:29 to 24:1	12 - 19
After the Resurrection	28	16	24	20 - 21

WHAT DID WE LEARN?

The four Gospels provide the testimony of four people who each have a different emphasis concerning the life and ministry of Jesus. The book of Acts gives the history of the early Christians and the spread of Christianity through the ministry of the apostles, focusing especially on Paul.

Lesson 6 - The Gospels and Acts

Activities

Time 20'

INSTRUCTIONS:

1. Why are the first three Gospels called the Synoptic Gospels?
___
___

2. Describe in your own words the advantages of having four Gospels.
___
___

3. What is your favorite passage from the Gospels and why it is so important to you? After answering, share your response with another student.
___
___

4. In groups of 3 or 4 persons, read Acts 2:43-47. Fill in the box below. Make a list of the characteristics that describe the lifestyle of this church and then evaluate the lifestyle of the people in your church using the following table:

1-4 low / 5-7 mediocre / 8-9 fairly good / 10 excellent

Lifestyle of an Exemplary Church	Evaluation of my Local Church

5. In the same groups, work together suggesting ideas that could improve those aspects in your church where the rating is lower.
___
___
___

Lesson 7

THE PAULINE EPISTLES

Objectives

- To learn the general content of the Pauline Epistles.
- To identify general aspects of each letter.
- To recognize the importance of Paul's teachings in today's context.

Ideas Principales

- The Apostle Paul was a Pharisee who converted to Christianity and was called as a missionary to the Gentiles.
- His letters give us practical advice for Christian living.
- The letters to Timothy and Titus contain instructions for pastors.

Introduction

Who was Paul? Previously, Paul was known by the name Saul of Tarsus. He was born between years 5 and 10 A.D. in Tarsus of Cilicia, which is located on the southern coast of Asia Minor (now Turkey) to a Jewish family of the tribe of Benjamin (Romans 11:1, Philippians 3:5). During his teen years he studied at the feet of the famous teacher Gamaliel (Acts 22:3). After the death of Jesus, about the year 33 A.D., Saul was an active persecutor of the community of disciples, following orders of the Jewish leaders. In fact, he participated in and approved the execution of Stephen (Acts 7).

In the year 36 A.D., according to the book of Acts and his own testimony in the Epistles, as he was on his way to Damascus to persecute Christians, Jesus Christ appeared to him and Saul converted to Christianity. Later he was baptized and from that moment on, Paul becomes a faithful follower of Christ and a preacher of the gospel. He was called "the apostle to the Gentiles" which is to say he was called to the non-Jews. He traveled as a missionary and established congregations in Greece, Asia Minor, Syria, Palestine, and he wrote letters to these churches.

He made three missionary journeys: on the first journey he evangelized the villages around Cilicia; the second, he toured the cities of Greece, especially Athens and Corinth; and in the third, he travelled to Greece, but focused his ministry in and around Ephesus. In the time of Emperor Nero, Paul was taken to Rome, where he used his incarceration in a rented house to share lessons with and strengthen the church in that city. He was released but arrested again later and was martyred.

His letters are recognized as the Pauline Epistles. Each is targeted to a particular church or person as in the case of the letter to Philemon. They were written during the first century with the purpose of encouraging the Christians of the churches he founded on his missionary journeys. The letters instruct believers on various doctrinal matters, about Christian lifestyle in the world and the organization and administration of the ministries of the church.

Paul: His name was Saul of Tarsus. He was born in the city of Tarsus, in the province of Cilicia (now Turkey) between 5 and 10 AD. He was about the same age as Jesus. Paul received the best education for a Jew of his time and was trained in Greek culture. He was a Pharisee, a Roman citizen and spoke several languages, which allowed him to carry the gospel throughout the Roman Empire. He was imprisoned and died in Rome in the year 65.

Gentile: *Term used by the Jews to refer to a person who was not Jewish.*

Classification of the Pauline Epistles (Letters):

Eschatological (about the end times)	Soteriological (about salvation)	Ecclesiological (about the church)	Pastoral
1 Thessalonians	Galatians	Ephesians	1 Timothy
2 Thessalonians	1 Corinthians	Colossians	2 Timothy
	2 Corinthians	Philemon	Titus
	Romans	Philippians	
Written during his second missionary journey	*Written during his third missionary journey*	*Written from prison in Rome*	*Written to Paul's fellow workers in ministry*

Cilicia: A Roman province of Asia Minor, located in what today is Turkey. It is the birthplace of Paul and one of the first Christian communities (Galatians 1:21).

Date and Content of the Pauline letters

In the New Testament there are thirteen letters written by Paul.

Romans: The central theme of this letter is justification by faith and sanctification through the Holy Spirit.

Date and Location: The Book of Romans was written during Paul's third missionary journey, sometime between 57-59 A.D. It was written in Corinth. Paul is the author, but a man named Tercio wrote the words on paper (Romans 16:22).

Purpose: Paul shows that all men, Jews and Gentiles alike, are condemned for their sins; he teaches that salvation is by faith and wrought by God's grace and not by law or works. He explains how God's grace is sufficient to bring every sinner to be a child of God and to live a holy life. It also provides a guide for the Christian life.

1 Corinthians: The main focus is on Christian conduct in relation to the church, the home and the world.

Date and location: This letter was probably written between 54 and 57 A.D. The location is Ephesus because according to Acts 20:31, Paul spent three years there. It was written to the church in Corinth.

Purpose: To lead the church in the midst of the difficulties they were experiencing. The Christians were divided by their fanatical personal adherence, some to Paul, some to Peter and others to Apollos, putting at serious risk the unity of the church. Paul also confronts the issue of those who were participating in rituals to other gods as part of the corrupt customs of the people of that city, bringing immorality to the forefront of the church. This issue needed immediate correction.

Content of Romans:
1. Doctrinal aspects (1:16 to 11:36)
2. Exhortations (12:1-15:13)

Content of 1 Corinthians:
1. Correction of moral and social issues (1-8)
2. Apostolic authority (9)
3. Order in the Church (10-14)
4. The Resurrection (15)
5. Conclusion (16)

Corinth: A city and rich commercial port in Greece. There were many merchants, craftsmen and Roman officials living there and two-thirds of the population were slaves. There was a mix of various cultures and many temples and shrines to different gods. The sanctuary of the goddess Aphrodite had over a thousand "sacred" prostitutes. It was a city famous for its vices and sins.

Lesson 7 - The Pauline Epistles

Philippi: An important city of Macedonia, on the road linking the east and west. It was famous for its gold mines.

The letter teaches that Christians are the church, which is the Body of Christ, and therefore, must abstain from the practice of sin that was part of the society in which they lived, and to separate themselves from anything that damages or contaminates. The letter also clarifies two issues: that the gifts received from the Spirit are given for the edification of the church, and that resurrection after death is guaranteed to the children of God.

2 Corinthians: The main theme of this letter is to give witness to the faithful ministry of Paul as an apostle: his motives, his dedication and his sufferings for the gospel.

Date and location: After sending his first letter to the Corinthians, Paul sent Timothy and then Titus to carry out certain reforms within the churches and to inform him of the effect of his letter. When Paul left Ephesus and went on to Macedonia, Titus came to meet him with an encouraging report about the conduct of the Corinthians. It was then that Paul wrote this second letter probably between the years 54 and 57 A.D. perhaps from the city of Philippi or from Ephesus, where Paul spent three years (Acts 20:31).

Purpose: The letter shows that there can be no communion between the church and the world and emphasizes the fact that the church is a creation of the Holy Spirit. The letter was written with a dual purpose: to comfort some who had been saddened by the contents of the first letter, and to defend his apostolic authority and character to those who criticized him.

Content of 2 Corinthians:
1. A Look Back (1:1-2-13)
2. The Dignity and Effectiveness of Paul's Ministry (2:14-7:1-16)
3. The Collection of the Offering (8-9)
4. Paul's Defense of his Apostleship (10:1-13:14)

Content of Galatians:
1. The Apostle of Freedom (1-2)
2. The Doctrine of Freedom (3-4)
3. The Life of Freedom (5-6)

Galatians: The central theme of the letter is the defense of the doctrine of justification by faith. Some believers doubted and wanted to return to the Jewish religion. Salvation in Judaism depended on obedience to the law of Moses. This was not correct according to the teaching of Jesus. Obedience to the law of Moses does not save, nor does it provide eternal life. Salvation comes only through faith in Jesus Christ. There was no need for circumcision, animal sacrifices or following the many Pharisaic laws to have forgiveness of sin.

Date and location: Galatians was written between the years 48 and 50 A.D. in Antioch to the church in Galatia.

Purpose: This letter presents the conflict between Judaism and Christianity. Paul refutes the teaching of some Jewish leaders who guided Christians to return to the "slavery of Pharisaic law" and to follow all its requirements, such as circumcision. Paul states that returning to this life denies the freedom we have in Christ. The letter teaches that the Christian is forgiven and received as a child of God by faith, not by meeting certain standards of conduct. The Holy Spirit had given new life (spiritual); therefore, the rituals of the Old Testament were no longer needed, but now the believers must live in holiness as Christ did.

Ephesus: The most important port city in the Roman province of Asia, located in what is present day Turkey.

Ephesians: The theme is the unity of the church and God's purpose for the church.

Date and location: Ephesians was written in Rome in 60-64 A.D.

Purpose: This letter teaches about the unity of the church, especially among Jewish and Gentile believers. God had determined that the Gentiles should be adopted as his sons and daughters, just like the Jews. The Gentiles now enjoyed the same blessings in Christ and together the Jews and Gentiles were one people, the people of God.

The unity of the Church as the body of Christ is the main subject of this letter, written in two sections: the doctrinal section, where the emphasis is on the spiritual blessings and the universal church (1-3) and the practical section where Paul teaches how the church must function (4-6).

Philippians: The central theme is having joy in life and Christian service, no matter the circumstances.

Date and location: This letter was written in Rome in 60-64 A.D. around the time of Paul's martyrdom.

Purpose: Paul expresses his gratitude for the love shown to him by the brethren in Philippi and for the gift that they sent. In this letter Paul teaches that Christians should have the same character as Christ, even in the midst of suffering, since Christ, humbly and willingly, gave Himself for us.

Colossians: This letter speaks against certain erroneous and dangerous teachings.

Date and location: This letter was written in Rome between 60-64 A.D. and was directed to the Colossian church in Asia Minor.

Purpose: This letter refutes the doctrinal errors arising from the mixture of teaching Judaism with Eastern religions and ideas that later in the second century would lead to Gnosticism, one of the greatest heresies that the church faced in its history. In the teachings of Gnosticism, it is claimed that to obtain salvation it is required to receive a higher knowledge revealed in secret to a privileged circle of people and that it is also necessary to live a rigorous life of abstaining from pleasures of the flesh, because the material world is evil and opposed to the spirit. A characteristic feature of these teachings was the worship of angels (2:18); it was believed that angels could free people from the limitations of the material and sinful body.

1 Thessalonians: The central issue in this letter is the second coming of Christ in relation to the encouragement, comfort, assurance and sanctification of the believer.

Date and location: Written in 51 A.D. in Corinth and Thessalonica.

Purpose: This is a personal letter where Paul seeks to encourage and reassure the Christians of Thessalonica, to thank God for the good news that has come from them and remind them of his desire to visit them soon. The letter urges them to live so that they please God. The letter responds to concerns concerning the coming of the Lord, for example, "When will He return? and "What will happen to the Christians who have died before his coming?" The letter ends with practical instructions, a prayer and greetings.

Content of Ephesians:
1. The call of the church (1-3)
2. Conduct in the church (4-6)

Content of Philippians:
1. Paul's situation and his work in the church (1)
2. Examples of self-denial (2)
3. Warning against errors (3)
4. Exhortations

Content of Colossians:
1. Greetings (1:1-12)
2. True doctrine (1:13-2:3)
3. False doctrine (2:4-23)
4. Required conduct (3:1-4:6)
5. Conclusion (4:7-8)

Apostasy: A Greek word meaning to fall into rebellion. Apostate: a person that decides after being a Christian to renounce his or her faith to return to a sinful lifestyle and to practice another religion.

Crete: A large island in the Mediterranean Sea, mostly mountainous, located in southeast Greece. It was the original land of the Philistines. Its inhabitants were known as liars and lazy gluttons (Titus 1:12).

Lesson 7 - The Pauline Epistles

Colosse: A city close to Laodicea (now Turkey) from which came a number of Paul's coworkers. It was a Christian community. It was destroyed by an earthquake in 65 A.D.

Content of 1 Thessalonians:
1. Hope for the recently converted (1)
2. Hope for the faithful servants of God (2)
3. Hope of purity for the believers (3:1 – 4:12)
4. Hope for the afflicted (4:13-18)
5. Warning to the sleeping Christians (5)

Content of 2 Thessalonians:
1. The persecuted Christians (1:1-7)
2. The unrepentant (1:8-12)
3. Apostasy (2:1-12)
4. Service (2:13 – 3:18)

Content of 1 Timothy:
1. Sound doctrine (1)
2. Prayer and advice to men and women (2)
3. Leadership and mission of the church (3)
4. Ministry of the church (4 – 6:10)
5. Concluding remarks (6:11-21)

Thessalonica: An important city in Macadonia (today's Greece), which was famous for its thermal baths, located in an important commercial route with a multicultural population. Paul founded a church there on his second missionary voyage. This area is now called Thessaloniki.

2 Thessalonians: The central theme is the second coming of the Lord in relation to persecuted believers, unrepentant sinners and the apostate church.

Date and location: The letter was written in the year 51-52 A.D. and sent from Corinth to Thessalonica.

Purpose: It is clear that certain expressions of the first letter of Paul to the church had been misinterpreted. When he had referred to the uncertainty of the day of the coming of Christ, his words had been understood as if he taught that the Lord's Day was near.

Paul writes for three reasons. First, he wanted to comfort believers under persecution. Second, he needed to correct a false teaching that the Lord's second coming had already occurred. (For this reason, the debates had started.) Third, he wanted to admonish some who were disorderly and refused to work while awaiting the coming of the Lord. In doing so, they took advantage of the charity of the church and demanded that the wealthier brothers care for them.

1 Timothy: The central theme is to describe the qualities and duties of the pastor, as well as his relations with the church, his family and society.

Date and location: This letter was probably written between 63 and 65 A.D. and was sent from Macedonia to Ephesus for Timothy.

Purpose: The letter was written to teach Timothy about ministry, to encourage him and to warn him against false teachers.

2 Timothy: The theme is to encourage Timothy to remain faithful to his calling in the face of obstacles.

Date and location: This letter was written between 67 and 68 A.D. and sent from Rome to Ephesus. It is generally believed that Paul was imprisoned in Rome twice and that this letter was written during his second imprisonment.

Purpose: To encourage and instruct a young pastor and teacher in his ministerial work.

Titus: The central issue is how to exercise spiritual leadership at several churches and what faithfulness to Christ looks like in the true church.

Date and location: Written between 63-65 A.D. and sent from Greece or perhaps Corinth to Crete for Titus, a Gentile who had accompanied Paul on several occasions.

Purpose: This letter focuses on the proper conduct of the spiritual leader who supervises and directs the work of several pastors and churches. The letter encourages Titus to instruct the Christian people in the truths of the gospel to bring them to spiritual maturity.

Philemon: The Epistle to Philemon is a short but powerful testimony about the transforming power that faith, forgiveness and freedom in Christ brings. This letter teaches that spiritual regeneration produces social justice.

Date and location: This letter was written between the years 60 and 62 A.D. and was sent from Rome to Colossae for Philemon.

Purpose: To appeal to the Christian named Philemon for Onesimus, a thief and a fugitive slave, who had now become a Christian and wanted to restart his life. Philemon was a member of the Colossian church, which probably met at a home. Paul begs Onesimus to forgive his new brother in Christ and receive him into his house as before.

Topics of the Pauline Letters

Romans	Salvation by faith
1 Corinthians	Speaks against divisions in the church
2 Corinthians	Paul defends his ministry
Galatians	Speaks against legalism
Ephesians	Unity in Christ
Philippians	Joy in the middle of suffering
Colossians	New life in Christ
1 and 2 Thessalonians	The second coming of Christ
1 Timothy and 2 Timothy	Advice for a young pastor
Titus	Instructions for the leaders in Crete
Philemon	Paul asks Philemon to receive Onesimus, a fugitive slave, as his brother in Christ.

Timothy: A young Christian whose father was Greek and his mother Jewish. Timothy probably converted during Paul's first trip to Lystra. He was a faithful coworker of Paul who trusted him to work in various assignments: Thessalonica, Corinth and elsewhere.

Content of 2 Timothy:
1. Greetings and exhortation (1)
2. Advice to the young servant of the Lord (2)
3. Predictions of apostasy and social corruption (3)
4. Final Orders (4)

Content of Titus:
1. The organization and discipline of the church (1)
2. Sound doctrine and good works (2)
3. Additional instructions (3)

Content of Philemon:
1. Greetings and praise (1:1-7)
2. Intercession for Onesimus (1:8-21)
3. Greetings and blessings (1:22-25)

What Did We Learn?

Paul wrote letters to the churches he founded in various cities of the empire with the purpose of teaching sound doctrine, teaching about the nature and organization of the church and to correct errors, sinful behaviors and habits among Christians and the Christian Church.

Titus: A Greek Christian disciple of Paul (Titus 1:4) and assistant in his missionary work. During the third missionary journey he was assigned work in Corinth (1 Corinthians 1-6 and 2 Corinthians 2:13, 7:5-16). Afterwards Paul left him in Crete to work with the churches there (Titus 1:4-5).

Activities

Time 20'

INSTRUCTIONS:

1. What aspect of the life and ministry of the Apostle Paul most impacts you?
___
___

2. In several of his letters, Paul teaches that the Church is the body of Christ. How would you explain this truth in your own words?
___
___
___
___

3. Compare the situation in the church of Corinth with the Christian churches in your context.
___
___
___
___

4. In many of his letters, Paul fought against twisted doctrines that brought up doubts and confusion among Christians. Can you mention some deceptive theologies that have spread in recent years? For example: prosperity theology.
___
___
___
___

5. According to Paul's instructions to Titus and Timothy, what was the responsibility of spiritual leaders concerning these teachings that divert and confuse the believers?
___
___
___
___

Lesson 8

THE GENERAL EPISTLES AND REVELATION

Objectives

- To understand the teachings of the General Epistles and Revelation.
- To value the message of these teachings in our times.
- To describe the general aspects of each book.

Ideas Principales

- The General Epistles or Catholic Epistles are called this because they have no definite or specific recipient.
- The Book of Revelation contains the revelation of Jesus Christ to the Apostle John about the end times and the Second Coming.

Introduction

Christian Ethics: *Ethics in general is the science that deals with determining what is good and right both personally as well as socially. Christian ethics is concerned with providing guidance on what is good and correct based on the teachings and values taught in the Bible.*

In addition to Paul's thirteen letters, the New Testament contains a series of letters written by other apostles. These letters are known as the General Epistles or Catholic Epistles because most of them do not have a clearly identified destination.

With the exception of 2 and 3 John where the recipients themselves are identified, the other letters are addressed to all the churches and so the teachings are more general. For example, James writes "to the twelve tribes scattered among the nations" (James 1:1), which refers to believers everywhere. Similarly 1 Peter is addressed "To God's elect, exiles scattered throughout the provinces of Pontus, Galatia, Cappadocia, Asia and Bithynia," meaning all the churches in those regions. For this reason the letters are named after the author rather than the names of the recipients.

In general, we can say that James and 1 Peter discuss topics related to Christian ethics and call believers to a holy walk with the Savior. The letters of 2 Peter and Jude are eschatological, warning believers about false teachers and encouraging them to defend the truth of the gospel. Hebrews and the Epistles of John are primarily Christological and ethical, calling Christians to abide in Christ, for He is the final revelation of God and the fulfillment of the Old Testament covenant.

Literary Aspects

Eschatology: *The term comes from the Greek and means "recent events." Christian eschatology is a branch of theology that studies the Biblical teaching on life after death and the events related to the Second Coming of Christ and the full establishment of the kingdom.*

The General Epistles contain doctrine and guidance for Christian living.

The General Epistles compliment the teaching of Pauline doctrine. In each of these letters, the apostles, who had been with the Lord during his ministry, reinforce and amplify the teachings of Paul, then relate these teachings to practical aspects related to the Christian life.

The theme of **Hebrews** is the superiority of the doctrine of Christ when compared to the covenant, the high priest, the sacrifice and the tabernacle.

Author and date: The letter is anonymous. It has been attributed to Paul, Barnabas, Luke and Apollos, among others. It was probably written between 60-70 A.D., and it is not known where it was written. It was addressed to a group of Jewish Christians of the first century who were apparently considering leaving the Christian faith.

Purpose: The letter was written in order to prevent Christians Jews from returning to Judaism.

The theme of the Epistle of **James** is practical religion, manifested in good works, in contrast to a mere statement of faith.

Author and date: The Apostle James served as one of the leaders of the church in Jerusalem. According to Josephus, James was killed by order of the Sanhedrin in 62 A.D. This letter was likely written between the years 40 and 50 A.D. in Jerusalem.

Purpose: James wrote this letter to encourage believers to live in obedience to the truth revealed in Jesus Christ and demonstrate their living faith through their attitudes and actions. James warns them that refusal to change their character and behavior is a symptom of a dead faith.

1 Peter: The central theme of this epistle is the victory over suffering as was exemplified in the life of Christ.

Author and date: This letter was written by the Apostle Peter, probably between 60 and 64 A.D., perhaps in Rome. It was written to Christians scattered throughout Asia Minor. It was likely written to the whole body of Christians in the region, both Jews and Gentiles.

Purpose: In writing this letter, Peter obeyed two specific orders that Jesus had given him: to give courage and strength to the brothers and to feed the flock of God. He encourages believers to stand firm during suffering, and he encourages them to live in holiness.

2 Peter is a warning about false teachers and unholy lifestyles.

Author and date: The Apostle Peter wrote this letter between the years 64-68 A.D., perhaps in Rome. The letter is addressed to a wide circle of Christians in the early church.

Purpose: In this second letter, Peter talks about the threat of false teachers who sought to corrupt the believers, both in doctrine and in practice.

1 John is a warning against false teaching and a call to bear witness through the practice of piety as a visible expression of faith.

Author and date: The Apostle John wrote this letter about 95 A.D. It was addressed to various Christian communities.

Purpose: The purpose of this letter is to show the character of God and to warn Christians about the enemies of Christ who teach false doctrines.

Lesson 8 - The General Epistles and Revelation

Content of Hebrews:
1. Superiority of Jesus (1-4)
2. Priesthood of Christ (5-10)
3. Basics of a better life (11-13)

Content of James:
1. True religion (1 and 2)
2. False Christianity (3 and 4)
3. Final teachings (5)

Content of 1 Peter:
1. The glorious salvation (1:1-21)
2. The believer's life in the light of salvation (1:21-2:8)
3. Position and duties of believers (2:9-3:13)
4. Instructions about suffering (3:14 to 4:19)
5. Exhortations and final warnings (5)

Content of 2 Peter:
1. The spiritual life (1)
2. False teachers and their doctrines (2)
3. About the Lord's Day (3)

Christological: *Doctrines of the Christian church regarding the nature of Christ, such as His eternal existence, His incarnation, His dual nature (divine and human), His deity, His role in salvation provided by God, among others.*

Piety: The Greek word is "eusebeia" which means "likeness to God." It is "a comprehensive term for the practice of Christian personal religion, the worship and service of God and the rendering of relevant obedience to his laws" (New Bible Dictionary, Marshall, 1996). Some Bible versions translate the Greek word as "holiness."

Content of 1 John:
1. The Incarnation (1:1-10)
2. The believer's life (2:1-4:6)
3. Love and the triumph of justice (4:7-5:5)
4. The assurance of eternal life (5:6-21)

Content of 2 John:
1. Greeting (1-3)
2. Commandment of love (4-6)
3. Faith in Christ (7-11)
4. Farewell (12-13)

Content of 3 John:
1. Greeting (1)
2. Praise of Gaius (2-8)
3. Behaviors opposed to Gaius (9-12)
4. Farewell (13-15)

Content of Jude:
1. Greeting (1:1-2)
2. Condemnation of heretics (1:3-23)
3. Final Praise (1:24-25)

2 John: The themes include love between Christians and true faith in Jesus Christ when confronting false teachers.

Author and date: The letter was written by the Apostle John probably between the years 75 and 85 A.D. It is addressed to "the elect lady and her children," which is believed to be a symbolic way to direct the letter to the churches.

Purpose: Like the previous letter, this letter warns about false teachers and their doctrines and calls for the believers to live in brotherly love in the community of faith.

3 John: The theme is hospitality towards God's servants and the danger of taking a tyrannical or authoritarian attitude like Diotrephes.

Author and date: The Apostle John wrote this letter at about the same time as the two previous letters.

Purpose: This is a letter that congratulates and encourages a particular brother in the faith to continue to be hospitable to those whom others reject. He warns that those who want to practice sound doctrine also should practice Christian hospitality with brothers in Christ.

The Epistle of **Jude** deals with the subject of the Christian's responsibility to guard against the sin of the world and to defend sound doctrine in the face of sinful teachings and practices.

Author and date: The author is disclosed as Jude, a servant of Jesus Christ and brother of the Apostle James. Since James was a blood brother to the Lord, it is implied that Judas the son of Mary is the Judas mentioned in Matthew 13:55 and Mark 6:3. No exact date has been set for the letter, but it would be after the fall of Jerusalem in the year 70 A.D.

Purpose: To warn about teachers who taught heresy or false teaching and to encourage the brothers to stand firm in the faith.

Topics of the General Epistles

Hebrews	The superiority of Christ
James	Faith without works is dead
1 Peter and 2 Peter	Hope in Jesus Christ
1 John, 2 John and 3 John	God is light and love
Jude	Teaches against false teachers
Revelation	Christ's final victory

The Book of Revelation

Revelation is the only prophetic book of the New Testament.

Revelation is a word of Greek origin meaning "to reveal, express or discover." It is an appropriate name for this book since it contains the visions that John received from Jesus Christ. Revelation belongs to the genre of apocalyptic prophetic literature, which is characterized by describing the story in a symbolic way. The Book of Revelation by John is Christian, but it includes many Jewish apocalyptic symbols found in the books of Daniel, Ezekiel and Zechariah.

In the Old Testament, apocalyptic literature encouraged Israel in times of national crisis, raising their hope for a Messianic triumph over their enemies. In this way, Ezekiel, for example, wrote during the siege and fall of the Southern Kingdom. Apocalyptic imagery and symbolism represent an objective reality with greater meaning than the images themselves. Apocalyptic literature of the Old and the New Testament provides a philosophy of history in symbolic form describing the ongoing struggle between good and evil in the world, with the assurance that although evil is rising, God and His people will triumph in the end.

The visions in Revelation are symbolic and are recounted in the style of a great drama unfolding in various acts and that takes place throughout the universe. The primary characters are the triune God, Satan, the Church and the enemies of the Church. Future events are described in which God's saving purpose for humanity triumphs over the forces of evil. The book continues the story to the end of history and beyond.

In the effort to understand the book, various schools of interpretation have arisen which seek to explain its meaning. John's extensive use of images and symbols has made interpretation difficult. Here are three of the ways that you can understand the book:

a. The preterist interpretation states that the book recounts events of John's day; therefore, it does not relate to our present day or to some future time. They claim that John describes the persecution suffered by Christians at the hands of various Roman emperors and therefore the book was written specifically to comfort the church during that time of persecution.

b. The futuristic interpretation emphasizes that most of the book is concerned with the future and the things described in it will happen before the Second Coming of Christ.

c. The historical interpretation considers that the purpose of the book is to show an overview of church history from the days of John until the end times. The book provides a series of stages that the church goes through up to the moment of the final victory.

Heresy: *a division or sect subject to its own leadership, who teach deviations from the original faith.*

Diotrephes: *No one knows for sure if he was a member of the church or a bishop, but he was a leader in the Asia Minor church who abused his authority. He refused to submit to any authority that was not his own. He gossiped about the Apostle Paul using malicious words. He rejected and even expelled from the church those who John sent to him to give counsel (3 John 9-10).*

Creed: *A brief, officially recognized statement summarizing the beliefs of the Christian church.*

Author and date: The book was written by the Apostle John, who presents himself as a prophet. There are two possible dates for the book. One date is around 65 A.D. at the time of the persecution of Christians by Nero. The other date is approximately 95 A.D. during the persecution of Domitian. The book was written on the island of Patmos, where John had been deported. The book is addressed to the churches of western Asia Minor during the first century, but the message is to the church in all places and at all times.

Purpose. To comfort and encourage Christians in the midst of persecution, both present and future, assuring them of the final triumph of Christ and his followers. The book warns the churches about the neglect of the doctrine or the experience of holiness. It is the only prophetic book of the New Testament, although in other books there are references to the Second Coming of the Lord and the end times.

The themes of Revelation are the Lord's Day, the judgment day, punishment for God's enemies and salvation and reward for those who are faithful. The message culminates with the announcement of the restoration of the city of God (the heavenly Jerusalem), the re-creation of the earth and the full restoration of the kingdom of Jesus Christ and His holy people.

Outline of the Book of Revelation

1. Foreword, 1:1-8

2. First vision, 1:9-3:22

    - 7 letters to the churches

3. Second Vision, 4:1-16:21

    -7 Seals (6:1-8:1)

    -7 Trumpets (8:2-14:20)

    -7 Visions of the dragon and his kingdom (12:1 - 13:18)

    -7 Bowls of wrath (15:1-16:21)

4. Third vision, 17:1-21:8

    -7 Visions of the fall of Babylon (17:1-19:10)

    -7 Visions of the end (19:11-21:8)

5. Fourth vision, 21:9-22:5

6. Epilogue, 22:6-21

Gaius: An elderly Christian man to whom John directs his third letter. It may be the same man who accompanied Paul on his journey to Ephesus (Acts 19:29).

Asia Minor: A region thus named by the Greeks, which included a large number of states. Its capital or main city was Ephesus. It is in present day Turkey.

Visions of John: The visions that John recorded in the book of Revelation are not merely a guess or a feeling of what might happen in the future. The prophetic vision is a means by which God reveals His will to the prophet. The vision can never go against the teaching of the Word (Acts 7:38, Romans 3:2). In the vision God allowed the prophet to "see" what others cannot in respect to certain events that will happen in the future (somewhat like a projection on a screen).

Comparative table: The message of prophecy and revelation		
Item	Prophecy	Revelation
1. Method used to reveal the message	The message is received primarily through speaking to the heart; it includes orders and disclosures that must be communicated; the visions are not the primary focus.	Revelations were received almost exclusively by visions or dreams.
2. Destination of the message	Rebellious people	Faithful people
3. Purpose of the message	To try to reform the sinner. To seek repentance in the people.	To raise hope in the eschatological intervention of God in human history.
4. Content of the message	- Promise of destruction and punishment to the rebels. - Evangelism: Salvation and the coming Messiah. - Seeing the hand of God in history and its end. - Reward to those who accept the Messiah.	The destruction of the wicked. The final triumph of Christ in history.

Patmos Island: A rocky, treeless place to which John was banished under the persecution of Emperor Domitian in 95 A.D. It is there that John had the visions of the Book of Revelation.

John: The son of Zebedee and Salome, and the brother of James the disciple. He was discipled by Christ and was called the beloved disciple. He wrote the Gospel of John and the Book of Revelation.

Lesson 8 - The General Epistles and Revelation

Contrast Between Genesis and Revelation		
GENESIS	HISTORY OF SALVATION	REVELATION
Beginning	Sin, separation from God	End
Paradise Lost	Formation of the People of God	Paradise Restored
Creation	Jesus Christ reconciles us with God	New Creation
First Man Sins	The Holy Spirit comes to live in the the children of God and teaches them to live in holiness	Man is Redeemed of Sin
Beginning of Sin	The Church, the first fruits of the new creation	The End of Evil
Promise of Redemption	The gospel is preached to all	Redemption Completed
Satan Enters (Satan loose)	Evil continues to grow	Judgment of Satan
Marriage of first Adam	The church makes disciples in all nations	Marriage of Second Adam
First Tears		All tears wiped away
Communion with God Interrupted		Communion Restored
God: The Sovereign Creator		God: Sovereign Ruler

WHAT DID WE LEARN?

The General Epistles bear the name of the authors and contain doctrinal teachings and guidance for Christian living. The book of Revelation is the last prophecy of the Bible in which Jesus Christ reveals to the Church the events that will bring about the final victory and where God's saving plan for his people will be specified. Christ's rule will be established and the re-creation of all things will restore everything to its original perfection.

Activities

Time 20'

INSTRUCTIONS:

1. What is meant by the term General Epistles?
_____
_____
_____

2. . The letter of James emphasizes that faith without works is dead. After reading 1:19-27, answer this question: Am I showing that my faith is alive through my actions?
_____
_____
_____
_____

3. How important is the study of the Book of Revelation to the church in our time?
_____
_____
_____
_____

4. Form 7 groups. Each group studies one of the letters to the churches referred to in Revelation chapters 2 and 3. (It there are not enaugh students, divide into 3 groups and each study 2 or 3 churches).

Each group completes the chart below for the assigned church and later share with the rest of the class.

Church Name	Symbolic Title	Qualities that are Praised	Criticism of Failures	Words of Promise	Teaching for my Church
EPHESUS					
SMYRNA					
PERGAMUM					
THYATIRA					
SARDIS					
PHILADELPHIA					
LAODICIA					

My Notes

Final evaluation

COURSE: THE BIBLE AND ITS MESSAGE

Name of Student: _____

Church or Study Center: _____

District: _____

Professor: _____

Date of this evaluation: _____

1. Explain in your own words how this course helped you to value the Bible.

_____
_____
_____
_____

2. Mention a course topic or lesson that was new and helpful to you. Explain why.

_____
_____
_____
_____

3. Explain how this course helped you to have a broader knowledge of the content of the Bible.

_____
_____
_____

4. What did you learn in the ministerial practice?

_____
_____
_____
_____

5. In your opinion, how could this course be improved?

_____
_____
_____

Bibliography

Books:

Alexander, David (comp). Manual Bíblico Ilustrado. Miami, Florida: Caribe. 1 edición, 1981.

Boyd, Frank. La Biblia a su Alcance. Tomos 3, 4, 5, 6, 7, 8. Miami, Florida: Editorial Vida, 1972.

Clyde T. Francisco. Introducción al Antiguo Testamento. El Paso, Texas. C. B. P., 1968.

Dana, H. E. El mundo del Nuevo Testamento. El Paso, Texas: C. B. P., 1970.

De Ausejo, Serafín. Diccionario de la Biblia. Barcelona: Herder, 1970.

Earle, Ralph. Cómo nos llegó la Biblia. Kansas City: C. N. P., 1975.

Earle, Ralph. Explorando el Nuevo Testamento. Kansas City: C. N. P., 1978.

Escobar, J.S. Padilla C.R., Yamauchi E.M. ¿Quién es Cristo hoy? Buenos Aires: Certeza. 1970.

Ellisen, Stanley A. Hacia el conocimiento del Antiguo Testamento. EEUU: Vida, 1990.

Evans, William. Esquema didáctico para el estudio de la Biblia. Barcelona: CLIE, 1990.

Francisco Clyde T. Introducción al Antiguo Testamento. El Paso: C. B. P., 1964.

Franco, Sergio. Aproximación al Estudio de la Biblia. Kansas, City: C. N. P., 1989.

Halley, H. Compendio Manual de la Biblia. EE.UU.: Moody, 1971.

Harrison, Everett. Introducción al Nuevo Testamento. Grand Rapids, Michigan: Libros Desafío, 1980.

Hester, H. I. Introducción al Nuevo Testamento. El Paso: C. B. P., 1963.

Hoff, Pablo. El Pentateuco. Deerfield, Florida: Vida, 1978.

_____ Libros históricos. Deerfield, Florida: Vida, s/f.

Lasor, William Sanford (et.al.). Panorama del Antiguo Testamento. Buenos Aires: Nueva Creación, 1995.

Lockward, Alfonso (Ed.). Nuevo Diccionario de la Biblia. Miami: Unilit, 1992.

Marshall, Howard I. The New Bible Dictionary. InterVarsity Press, 3rd Edition, 1996.

Mears, Henrietta. Lo que nos dice el Nuevo Testamento. Miami, Florida:Vida, 1979

Packer, James. La vida diaria en los tiempos bíblicos. Miami: Florida:Vida, 1982

Pearlman, Myer. A Través de la Biblia Libro por Libro. Miami,Florida:Vida, 1952.

Pietrantonio, Ricardo. Itinerario Bíblico.Vol 1. Buenos Aires: La Aurora, 1985.

Purkiser, W.T. Explorando el Antiguo Testamento. Kansas City: C. N. P., 1986.

Rand, W. El Diccionario de la Santa Biblia. San José, Costa Rica: Caribe, s/f

Sánchez, Edesio. ¿Qué es la Biblia?. Buenos Aires: Kairós, 2003.

Sánchez, Edesio (Ed). Descubre la Biblia. EE.UU. Sociedades Bíblicas Unidas, 1998.

Taylor, Richard S. (Ed.). Diccionario Teológico Beacon. Kansas City: C.N.P., 1995.

Tenney, Merrill. Nuestro Nuevo Testamento. Grand Rapids, Michigan: Portavoz, 1973.

Trenchard, Ernesto. Introducción al estudio de los cuatro evangelios. Inglaterra: Literatura Bíblica, s.f.

Ugalde, Carlos. Introducción al Antiguo Testamento. Material no editado.

_____ Introducción al Nuevo Testamento. Material no editado.

Vine, W.E. Diccionario Expositivo de palabras del Antiguo y Nuevo Testamento exhaustivo de Vine. Nasville, Tennessee: Grupo Nelson, 2007.

Wegner, Paul. *The Journey from Texts to Translations*. Baker Academic, 1999.

Yates, Kyle M. Los profetas del Antiguo Testamento. El Paso, Texas: C. B. P., 4ta. edición, 1981.

Web Pages:

Varetto, Juan C. La Biblia del oso. Sociedades Bíblicas Unidas. Recuperado el 20 de abril 2010 de http://labibliaweb.com/la-biblia-del-oso.

Studylight, *Holman Bible Dictionary*, accessed September 19, 2013. http://www.studylight.org/dic/hbd/

www.ingramcontent.com/pod-product-compliance
Lightning Source LLC
Chambersburg PA
CBHW081018040426
42444CB00014B/3265